T0215334

# PROGRAMMING BASICS

## GETTING STARTED WITH JAVA, C#, AND PYTHON

*Robert Ciesla*

Apress®

*Programming Basics: Getting Started with Java, C#, and Python*

Robert Ciesla
HELSINKI, Finland

ISBN-13 (pbk): 978-1-4842-7285-5 ISBN-13 (electronic): 978-1-4842-7286-2
https://doi.org/10.1007/978-1-4842-7286-2

Managing Director, Apress Media LLC: Welmoed Spahr
Acquisitions Editor: Shiva Ramachandran
Development Editor: James Markham
Coordinating Editor: Jessica Vakili

Distributed to the book trade worldwide by Springer Science+Business Media New York, 1 New York Plaza, New York, NY 100043. Phone 1-800-SPRINGER, fax (201) 348-4505, e-mail orders-ny@springer-sbm.com, or visit www.springeronline.com. Apress Media, LLC is a California LLC and the sole member (owner) is Springer Science + Business Media Finance Inc (SSBM Finance Inc). SSBM Finance Inc is a **Delaware** corporation.

For information on translations, please e-mail booktranslations@springernature.com; for reprint, paperback, or audio rights, please e-mail bookpermissions@springernature.com.

Apress titles may be purchased in bulk for academic, corporate, or promotional use. eBook versions and licenses are also available for most titles. For more information, reference our Print and eBook Bulk Sales web page at http://www.apress.com/bulk-sales.

Any source code or other supplementary material referenced by the author in this book is available to readers on GitHub via the book's product page, located at www.apress.com/978-1-4842-7285-5. For more detailed information, please visit http://www.apress.com/source-code.

Printed on acid-free paper

*Dedication*

*Thank you to the Association of Finnish Non-fiction Writers for their support in the production of this book.*

# Contents

About the Author............................................... vii

About the Technical Reviewer.................................. .ix

Chapter 1:   Wet Toes: The Very Basics of Programming ............. 1

Chapter 2:   Java, C#, and Python 101............................. 13

Chapter 3:   Setting Up Your Programming Environments ........... 29

Chapter 4:   Object-Oriented Programming (OOP) ................. 43

Chapter 5:   File Operations, Multithreading, and Other Wonders
             of Java ............................................. 63

Chapter 6:   And Now for Something Completely Different:
             Advanced Python ..................................... 85

Chapter 7:   Calendars, Culture, and Multithreading in C# .......... 107

Chapter 8:   Graduation Day: Slightly Larger Programming
             Projects ............................................ 129

Chapter 9:   UML Class Diagrams................................. 145

Index ......................................................... 167

# About the Author

**Robert Ciesla** is an author and filmmaker from Helsinki, Finland. He is also a freelance-programmer working mostly in the indie game scene. Robert is the author of *Encryption for Organizations and Individuals* (2020), *Game Development with Ren'Py* (2019), and *Mostly Codeless Game Development* (2017).

Visit www.robertciesla.com for more information. (image © by A.C. in 2021)

# About the Technical Reviewer

**Apoorv Gupta** is a Software Engineer in New York. He has worked on several subscription products at Youtube and Google Workspace. He enjoys hiking, snowboarding and advising startups.

# Wet Toes: The Very Basics of Programming

What do video games, social networks, and your activity bracelet have in common? They run on software a group of (more or less) programmers wrote somewhere far, far away. Gadgets and hardware are only one, more visible side of the coin of our technology-driven societies. In this chapter, we'll discuss the very basics of programming. We'll also take a gander at the visible parts of digital systems: the hardware.

## What Is Programming Anyway?

Basically, programming is the act of telling digital devices, such as your personal computer, what to do. We type in listings of commands, as defined by a programming language, in order to have useful or entertaining events occur. Properly programmed computers run much of the communications and online services in the world. You can mention things like ATMs, ticket readers, and smart phones as gadgets that run on software that somebody created in some programming language.

© Robert Ciesla 2021
R. Ciesla, *Programming Basics*, https://doi.org/10.1007/978-1-4842-7286-2_1

# Basic Hardware Rundown

As a budding programmer, you'll benefit from understanding the kind of universally found electronics you're working with. It's a good idea to have at least a basic understanding of the most commonly found components inside a computer.

These hardware components in a computer represent your work force. As a programmer, you run this show. Think of the act of programming as telling the factory workers what to build. You manufacture applications, whether they be big, complicated software projects or tutorials from some awesome book on coding.

---

For the purposes of this book, any relatively modern desktop or laptop computer works fine. We won't be needing any expensive hardware while getting our feet wet in programming.

---

# 1. Central Processing Unit (CPU)

Naturally, a digital device can't run on software alone; a **central processing unit (CPU)** is the hardware "brain" which executes code and makes things actually happen (see Figure 1-1). Even in a less complicated piece of electronics, all instructions flow toward and through a CPU (or a bunch of them). Being very small in size, these microchips have increasingly been a part of our lives since the 1970s. Every digital device has a CPU in it, probably even your stationary bicycle/ clothes rack.

**Figure 1-1.** A top-down view of an older Intel "Pentium 4" CPU used in millions of PCs back in 2005. Image by Eric Gaba. CC BY-SA 3.0

# 2. Hard Drives (a.k.a. Hard Disks)

This component is there to store data just about permanently. Within a hard drive, you'll find tens of thousands of files, whether they be pictures, text files, or databases. Your operating system (e.g., Windows or macOS), too, rests within the confines of a hard drive. These devices come in two varieties: *mechanical hard drives* (see Figure 1-2) and *solid state disks (SSDs)*.

**Figure 1-2.** A top-down view of a Western Digital mechanical hard drive. Image by "Darkone." Licensed under CC BY-SA 2.5 (creativecommons.org/licenses/by-sa/2.5/deed.en)

Mechanical drives are more affordable, but since they have moving parts inside, they are somewhat more easily damaged than SSDs by excessive vibration and extreme weather. In addition, solid state disks usually operate much faster.

# 3. Video Card

*Video cards* are responsible for displaying a system's visuals, whether they be plain text or dazzling 3D graphics in a modern video game. These devices come in a variety of configurations and prices, ranging from $30 word processor fiends to $1000 gaming monsters (see Figure 1-3). Computer monitors are typically connected directly to a video card.

**Figure 1-3.** An Nvidia 7900GS video card from 2006

The video card business has basically been a duopoly between *Nvidia* and *AMD,* two multibillion tech giants, ever since the early 2000s. However, Intel is making gains in this sector as well.

# 4. Random Access Memory (RAM)

*Random access memory*, commonly called RAM, is used as a computer's temporary storage. Physically it most often comes in the form of stick-like add-ons (see Figure 1-4). When running any type of software, your computer uses RAM to execute it from. Switching off your device will clear out your RAM. By contrast, data written on hard drives isn't erased when powering off a computer. Save your documents on a regular basis.

**Figure 1-4.** A typical stick of RAM. Image by Henry Kellner. CC BY-SA 4.0. Source: upload.wikimedia.org/wikipedia/commons/3/32/DDR3_RAM_53051.jpg

As of 2021, 4 GB (i.e., *four gigabytes*) is an adequate amount of RAM to have for most uses. Power users, such as video editors, will benefit from having 16 GB of RAM or more.

# 5. Motherboard

All of the aforementioned four hardware components (i.e., the CPU, the video card, the hard disks, and RAM) come together at the motherboard to create a working computer unit. The motherboard also has connectors for keyboard, mice, and other control devices (see Figure 1-5).

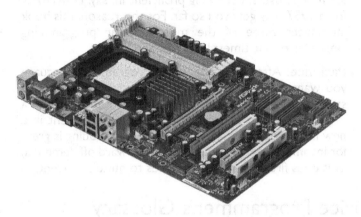

**Figure 1-5.** A modern PC motherboard. Image by Evan-Amos. CC BY-SA 3.0. Source: upload.wikimedia.org/wikipedia/commons/0/0c/A790GXH-128M-Motherboard.jpg

# The Three Requirements of Becoming a Decent Programmer

Let's next discuss some personal priorities all programmers should have in order to advance in their craft, whatever their starting level might be:

1.  **Self-confidence**: Ask yourself this, why do you want to learn to code? Some perfectly valid answers include "For professional development," "To maintain my faculties," and "I want to be a part of something great." Now, programming is sometimes considered a frightening activity by laypeople. It does take some guts to sit down, tune out, and enter the world of bit manipulation. Just remember that you, too, can achieve competence in this field, even if you're a complete beginner. Confidence comes from experience. Line by line you will obtain more good vibes and gain independence from programming books and online tutorials.

2. **The right language**: Not all of us benefit from becoming fluent in Esperanto or Classical Latin. When learning a new language, we tend to go for something useful, such as Spanish or French. Similarly, choosing a programming language which best suits your intentions is of paramount importance. If you want to eventually code recipe apps for mobile users, becoming proficient in, say, FORTRAN from 1957 only gets you so far. For this reason, this book introduces three of the most popular programming languages of our times: Java, C#, and Python.

3. **Patience**: After choosing which programming language you want to specialize in, you quite simply just have to stick to it. It takes anything between six months and a year of hands-on experience to become proficient in a new language. This is actually good news. Coding is great for insomnia and boredom. It may also ward off dementia, as it does fire those brain synapses to quite an extent.

# A Novice Programmer's Glossary

We'll now delve into some essential terminology related to the hallowed hobby of coding. There are hundreds of terms and concepts related to the various programming techniques and languages available. However, we'll only be focusing on the most relevant associated keywords, and in no particular order.

# Input/Output

*Input* in the context of programming refers to us entering data for a piece of software running on a computer to process. This comes in the form of typed text, mouse commands, or various types of files. For example, a word processing program (e.g., Microsoft Office) most often takes its input mostly as alphanumerical data provided by keystrokes. *Output* refers to data that has been processed by software. In a word processor this usually refers to a file document saved with the program. Such output can also be directed at printers or other devices. The output from programmers (carbon dioxide and other things notwithstanding) is typically a working application, whether it's a completed tutorial file or a bigger project.

# Algorithm

A working program listing basically constitutes an *algorithm,* which refers to a set of steps created to solve problems. Most software consists of numerous sub-algorithms. In the case of, say, a video game, there are algorithms for displaying graphics, saving and loading the game state, and playing audio files to name just a few.

# Flowchart

Programming projects and their algorithms are often visualized using *flowcharts,* especially in a team environment. These are a great way to demonstrate basic program flow in most instances.

Flowcharts consist of only a few universal elements (see Figure 1-6). In their most fundamental form, they use four symbols. These are the *terminal* (rounded rectangle), the *process* (rectangle), the *decision* (diamond/rhombus), and the *flowline* (arrowhead). The terminal symbol is used to denote the beginning and the end of a program flow. Any operations and general data manipulation are represented by process rectangles.

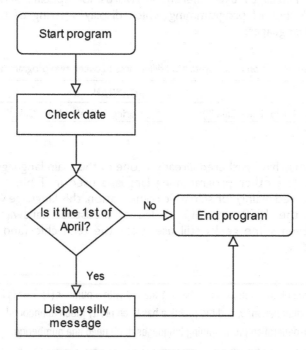

**Figure 1-6.** A very simple flowchart describing a program for April fools

Flowcharts are interpreted from top to bottom and left to right in most cases. *The American National Standards Institute (ANSI)* created the standards for flowcharts and their symbols back in the 1960s. This set of symbols has been expanded on during the 1970s and 1980s by the *International Organization for Standardization (ISO)*. For the purposes of this book, we'll stick to the originals.

# Source Code

This term refers to the collection of the more or less typed-in programming listings each software project is made of. As a programmer, you are a creator of *source code*. Simple programs come in the form of a single piece of source code, whereas complicated software, such as operating systems (e.g., Windows), potentially consists of tens of thousands of listings all constituting a single product.

# Syntax

A *syntax* is a set of rules and principles that govern the structure of sentences in a given language, including in the context of programming. Different programming languages use different keywords for specific actions. Now, behold actual lines of programming which display a string of text in two programming languages:

**Table 1-1.** A demonstration of the syntactical differences between two programming languages

| Java | FORTRAN |
| --- | --- |
| System.out.print("Hello! I like Cake!"); | 1 print *, "Hello! I like Cake!" |

Java, like you may have gathered already, is one of the main languages featured in this book. The other programming language used in Table 1-1 is called *FORTRAN*. Devised mainly for scientific computation, this language was created way back in the 1950s by IBM. A lot of industrial hardware runs on FORTRAN. Even some geeks still use it for the tech chic (and to a small extent, so did we).

---

You may notice one of our examples in Table 1-1 started with a number (1). This is known as a *line number* in coding parlance, and the practice has been pretty much abandoned a while ago. As a rule, current-generation programming languages don't need line numbering.

---

# Routine

A *routine* in the context of programming is a term for code which does a specific task and is intended to be summoned repeatedly at will by the coder. For example, a program may contain a simple routine for playing a sound effect. Instead of writing and rewriting the code each time said sound effect is needed, the programmer will trigger the same code (i.e., the routine) ad hoc.

---

Depending on the context and the programming language in use, a routine is sometimes also referred to as *a sub-routine, a function, a procedure,* or a *method.* We'll address the nomenclature in more detail later in this book.

---

# File Formats

A *file format* is a method of encoding data. By 2021, you've encountered many a file format already in your daily life. Digital photographs, love letters typed in OpenOffice, and those sassy Excel spreadsheets all represent different file formats. An image file (e.g., *apress_is_great.jpg*) resting on one's hard drive can only be used with software that deciphers it the way it was intended to, as an image. Similarly, opening *love-letter.doc* in a photo-editing suite would not provide you with optimal results, displaying gibberish at best. Most operating systems associate different available file formats with the right software, so you can safely double-click files and expect them to load up just fine.

# ASCII

*American Standard Code for Information Interchange (ASCII)* is a character-encoding standard that assigns letters, numbers, and other characters for use in computing and other digital equipment. In essence, what you are reading now is ASCII code. As a programmer, you'll come across the term rather frequently. An "ASCII file" is often used as a shorthand for "human-readable text file." The system dates back to 1963.

---

On the Internet of today, the most commonly used character-encoding standard is the UTF-8, which includes all of the ASCII alphanumericals as well as many other symbols.

---

# Boilerplate Code

The term *boilerplate* refers to programming code which is more or less automatically inserted into a program, needing little to no editing. When you start a new project in, say, a C++ environment, current-generation development tools will usually set you up with the necessary boilerplate code needed to run the program. If not, you can relatively safely copy-paste boilerplate code from your older working projects right into your new one to get started.

# Software Framework

A *software framework* **is a set** of generic functionalities which typically spare the coder a lot of time. There's no reason to reinvent the wheel, especially in software projects. A framework includes various software libraries of various focus, including file manipulation routines, audio playback, and 3D graphics routines (in the case of 3D video game development and other highly visual applications).

---

For the purposes of this book, we won't be delving deep in any complicated software frameworks, but it's important you understand the concept.

---

# Full Stack

A *full stack* is the software that makes up a fully working web application, such as an online database. A web application is often divided into two areas: a *front end* and a *back end*. The front end is made for the user; it contains all the user interface elements needed to use the app. The back end consists of web servers, frameworks, and databases. A *full stack developer* is therefore someone who knows their way across both the front end and the back end of online application coding.

# In Closing

Finishing this chapter you'll have hopefully gained some understanding of the following:

- The basic five hardware components in a computer
- The three main requirements for becoming a programmer
- Some essential programming concepts, including source code, syntax, and boilerplate code
- What flowcharts refer to and what their basic building blocks are

# Java, C#, and Python 101

In this chapter, we'll get acquainted with three of the most popular programming languages in 2021 (and probably beyond). Several concepts related to programming will be presented and discussed in some detail. These terms may seem daunting and/or clunky at first, but be aware they are actually rather simple once grasped and offer a special path straight into your computer's very heart. We'll begin by introducing you to these three amazing languages: Java, C#, and Python.

## Java

Created by *Sun Microsystems* and released in 1995, Java quickly became a widely adopted general-purpose programming language especially for online environments (i.e., cloud computing). Today, software written with Java powers countless smartphones, data centers, and ubiquitous online services like Google. As of 2021, it's among the most popular programming languages out there for novices and seasoned coders alike.

© Robert Ciesla 2021

R. Ciesla, *Programming Basics*, https://doi.org/10.1007/978-1-4842-7286-2_2

Although the programming language known as *JavaScript* shares its first four letters with Java, these two have very little in common. JavaScript was created by Internet pioneers *Netscape* back in the nineties for use with then-new browser technology. The language is still alive and well on the Internet, providing extra functionality and usability for a myriad of websites.

# C#

C# (pronounced C sharp) was released to the public in the summer of 2002. Developed by Microsoft, the language can be used to create any type of modern application from productivity software to video games. C# shares some of its features with several other popular programming languages including Java.

You may have heard of C++, which is an earlier and somewhat more complex language compared to C#. Although C++ is capable of producing more efficient output in general, with C#, it's more straightforward to develop mobile and web apps. As for the grandparent of both C++ and C#? Say hello to C (sometimes also called *Procedural C*), a language dating back to 1972.

# Python

Taking its name from *Monty Python,* a popular light entertainment TV show, Python was released in 1991. While Python's output is often slower than software made with C#, Python has nonetheless become quite popular in recent years. It can handle pretty much anything from making simple apps for the Web to heavier desktop software. Python has even found a niche in the video games industry for game prototyping purposes.

What's noteworthy about Python is the way it's sensitive to whitespaces/indentation (the invisible characters created by pressing the space bar and/or the tab key). We'll touch on this unique approach and more later in the book.

# Ones, Zeros, and You

Now, you may have heard the spiel on binary digits and how computers love it. And yes, on the most fundamental level, microprocessors do chew on ones and zeros (they really dig strings like, say, 01011010110). This closest level fed into central processing units is called the level of *machine language* or *machine code.* There are several layers of abstraction on top of this binary level to help us humans do our thing with computers.

Now, in programming, there's a distinction between *high-level* and *low-level* *languages*. This has nothing to do with the quality of the tools. This classification refers to how close to machine code (i.e., binary) a programming language is working on. Basically, high-level languages are closer to human language, while lower-level ones tend to look rather obscure to laypeople. C# and Python are considered high-level languages, while C++ represents what is known as a middle-level language as it offers some pretty solid features for more advanced programmers.

---

Wait, are you getting angsty at this point? Don't worry: in this book we'll focus on the high-level stuff only. Deeper knowledge of binary/machine code is not needed.

---

# Compiling and Interpreting Code

Computers can't execute any programming languages right off the bat. For example, Java and Python are both so-called interpreted languages. This means every line in a listing is "interpreted" into machine code in real time, step by step, as it happens. The process of interpretation tends to show in programs as slower execution speed compared to the other type of languages: the compiled variety.

Listings in *compiled languages* need to undergo a process called (you guessed it) *compiling* before being able to run. This refers to the translation of a program's full source code into machine language prior to its execution. Thankfully the compiling process is automated, so you don't need any programmer-to-machine code translation booklets. It's a function of any good coding development environment. See Table 2-1 for a rundown for the main differences between compiled and interpreted programming languages.

**Table 2-1.** The main differences between compiled and interpreted languages

| | Compiled language | Interpreted language |
|---|---|---|
| Examples | *C#, C++, C* | *Java, Python, JavaScript* |
| Main differences | • Entire code listing is translated into machine code (i.e., compiled) prior to execution | • Code is translated into machine code one step at a time in real time |
| | • Compilation time slows down development | • Quick to prototype |
| | • Builds faster software | • Builds slower software |
| | • Platform specific (Windows, macOS, Linux, etc.) | • Platform independent, near universal compatibility |
| | | • Great for online apps |

# The Magic of Variables

Variables are a form of temporary storage, available for the user of a program during the time they spend at a piece of software. Variables typically use the *random access memory (RAM)* in your device. This means if you switch off the power on your device, the data stored in variables disappears, unless it's saved to a storage device like a hard disk first.

A variable might be used to store the name of the player in a game, to name but one rudimentary usage scenario. From a programmer's point of view, variables are used and reused throughout a program. They can have multiple operations applied on them, from basic arithmetic to complicated mathematical formulations.

There are numerous types of variables in each programming language. In fact, there are separate variable types for strings of text, single alphanumerical characters, and different ranges of numeric values. But why make these distinctions? Well, sometimes all you need to store is a single character, say, the letter "B." It would be a waste of a computer's memory to reserve a type of variable space meant for 19-digit numeric values in the aforementioned scenario, hence the several varieties of variable types in most programming languages.

Many programming languages do not feature universal variables which can store any type of information. In most cases, the programmer needs to define *variable declarations* before use.

---

Computers aren't great with guessing. Most programming languages would make a clear distinction between the strings *happy_variable* and *Happy_Variable*. If a listing isn't working, it's possible there are simply some issues with capitalization.

---

# Variables in Python

Python has six core types of data types: *numbers*, *strings*, *lists*, *tuples*, *sets*, and *dictionaries*. Unlike Java and C#, in Python variables don't often require type declarations. You simply assign a value and its type is set automatically. See Table 2-2 for a rundown on these data types.

**Table 2-2.** The six main data types in Python

| Data type | Description | Example definitions |
|---|---|---|
| *Number* | Numbers in Python include integers (whole numbers), floating points, and complex numbers. Calculations can be done at the time of creating definitions | pie_diameter = 21<br>LuckyNumber = 5 + 1<br>Donut_Diameter = 6.26 + 0.11 |
| *String* | Strings are contiguous sets of alphanumerical characters. Both single and double quotes are accepted in their definitions | name = 'Sir Reginald of Sodbury'<br>nickname = "Reg"<br>Color = "Purple" |
| *List* | A list consists of values/variables of any type. Enclosed in square brackets, lists take single quotes with string values | jolly_list = [ 1, 2, 3, 4, 5 ]<br>happy_list = [ 'Hello', 123, 'Orange' ] |
| *Tuple* | Unlike lists, tuples are read-only and cannot be updated on the fly. Tuples are enclosed with parentheses | decent_tuple = ( 1, 2, 3 )<br>amazing_tuple = ( 1.12, "Ok," 456.5 ) |
| *Set* | A set is a collection of unordered values initialized using curly brackets. In sets, duplicate values are discarded | Fine_Animals = { 'Cat', 'Bat', 'Bat', 'Bird' }<br>three_great_numbers = { 1, 2, 3, 3, 3 } |
| *Dictionary* | Dictionaries are unordered key-value pairs, enclosed by curly brackets | Friends = { 'name': 'Yolanda', 'age': 25 }<br>cars = { 'make': 'Pinto', 'safety-level': 'great' } |

# Trying Out Python

You don't actually need to install any specific software to try out some basics of Python, C#, and Java programming. There are great online programming environments for experimentation in these languages. Now would be a great time to visit some of these services and frolic with Python's variables, for one. Try these out and stick to the one you like best:

- **Programiz Python Online Compiler**: www.programiz.com/python-programming/online-compiler

- **Online GDB Python Compiler**: www.onlinegdb.com/
  online_python_compiler

- **Repl.it Python Compiler**: https://repl.it/languages/
  python3

Ready to compile your first lines of Python? Fire up one of the online compilers and type Listing 2-1 into the programming space. Be prepared to remove the "hello world" listing, which is probably there by default. When you're done typing, click *Run* or *Execute* in the compiler interface to see the results.

**Listing 2-1.** *Notice how text (i.e., "My favorite beasts") can be displayed next to a variable using a comma in Python*

```
Fine_Animals = { 'Cat', 'Bat', 'Bat', 'Bird' }
print("My favorite beasts:", Fine_Animals)
```

In Listing 2-1, we first define a variable, *Fine_Animals,* which is a suitable name for our purposes. We then continue to use the print command to output its contents. This output should say *My favorite beasts: {'Bat', 'Cat', 'Bird'}* (perhaps in varying order). What happened to the second "bat"? It disappeared, because we defined a Python set data structure (familiar from Table 2-2) in which duplicate entries are not allowed.

# Manipulating Variables

There are many ways to manipulate values in variables. All basic arithmetic (i.e., addition, subtraction, multiplication, division, exponentiation, and extraction of roots) is covered in any programming language. The next small listing demonstrates this in Python. Clear your compiler programming space, and type in Listing 2-2 if you want to see it in action.

**Listing 2-2.** *The variable used is in bold*

```
favorite_number = 21
print("My favorite number is", favorite_number)
favorite_number+=2
print("No, it was", favorite_number)
favorite_number-=1
print("Wait.. it's actually", favorite_number)
```

---

In Listing 2-2, we used *addition* and *subtraction assignment operators* for our arithmetic purposes (i.e., += and -=). The following would've had the same result with our addition statement: *favorite_number = favorite_number + 2*

---

# Typecasting in Python

Some scenarios require a program to interpret certain values as specific variable types. This might be needed in cases where the user is expected to input an exact variety of data types. The process for converting from one data type to another is known as *typecasting* or *type conversion*. Luckily Python allows us to do just that using some rather simple methods.

Now, there are two types of typecasting: *implicit* and *explicit*. You might already be somewhat familiar with the former. Implicit typecasting simply refers to Python deducing the type of variable from the input you first assign to it (e.g., a number or a string of characters). In this section, we'll focus on explicit typecasting, in which a programmer assigns not just the value into a variable but also converts its data type into another. See Table 2-3 for some core typecasting functions in Python.

**Table 2-3.** Some explicit typecasting functions in Python

| Typecast | Function call | Example of use |
|---|---|---|
| Any type → integer | *int( )* | phone_number="5551234"<br>new_variable=**int(phone_number)**<br>print(new_variable) |
| Any type → floating point | *float( )* | wholenumber=522<br>floatnumber=**float(wholenumber)**<br>print(floatnumber) |
| Integer or float → string | *str( )* | float_variable=float(2.15)<br>string_variable=**str(float_variable)**<br>print(string_variable) |
| String → list | *list( )* | greeting="Hello"<br>a_list=**list(greeting)**<br>print(a_list) |
| String → set | *set( )* | fruit="Banana"<br>a_set=**set(fruit)**<br>print(a_set) |

# Variable Comparisons

There are other ways of utilizing a variable's contents, of course. To make usable software, we often need to compare values. There are six universal operators for this (see Table 2-4). These operators work for practically all programming languages, including the three featured in this book.

**Table 2-4.** The main comparison operators in Java, C#, Python, and most other languages

| Operator name | Operator symbol | Examples of use |
|---|---|---|
| Equal to | == | if (name == "Johnny") ... |
| Not equal to | != | if (age != 21) ... |
| Less than | < | if (age < adult_age) ... |
| More than | > | if (energy > max_energy) ... |
| Less than or equal to | <= | if (pet_snakes <= allowed_snake_amount) ... |
| More than or equal to | >= | if (gold >= 1000) ... |

Let's now peek at Listing 2-3 for a demonstration on how some of these comparisons work in Python.

**Listing 2-3.** *A simple listing in Python demonstrating comparison operators*

```python
print('Enter a number:')
YourNumber = input()
YourNumber = int(YourNumber)

if YourNumber > 10:
    print('Your number is greater than ten')
if YourNumber <= 10:
    print('Your number is ten or smaller')
```

# Variable Declarations in Java and C#

Now we move on to variables in the context of Java and C#. Unlike Python, these programming languages require that we define a variable's data type manually. For a detailed rundown on some of the main variable types in Java and C#, see Table 2-5. As you can see, for the most part, the variable type declarations are identical for both of these languages.

**Table 2-5.** The main variable types and their declarations for Java and C#

| Variable type | Java and C# | Variable range |
|---|---|---|
| Integer (whole numbers) | *int* | From -2,147,483,648 to 2,147,483,647 |
| Character | *char* | Single alphanumerical character (e.g., B) |
| Floating-point number | *float* | Fractional numbers between 6 and 9 decimals |
| Double floating-point number | *double* | Fractional numbers up to 17 decimals |
| Boolean (logical operator) | *bool* | True or false (i.e., one or zero) |
| String of text | *String (Java), string (C#)* | Arbitrary number of alphanumerical characters |

# Trying Out Java and C#

Not just limited to covering Python, several online compilers exist for both Java and C#. The following is a selection for your choosing pleasure. Pick a favorite so you can try out some live coding in these languages, too.

- **Jdoodle Java Compiler**: `www.jdoodle.com/online-java-compiler`

- **Paiza.io Java Compiler**: `https://paiza.io/projects/fjCEFnDQzDWOoS9hYZtVtg?language=java`

- **Dotnet Fiddle C# Compiler**: `www.dotnetfiddle.net`

- **Rextester C# Compiler**: `https://rextester.com`

# On Curly Brackets, Variable Scope, and Code Blocks

You'll come across several code listings with curly brackets soon in this chapter. They are indeed an important element in many programming languages. What these curly characters do is they denote *code blocks,* which consist of grouped declarations and/or statements. A compiler or interpreter software reads a single code block as a single instruction.

Also, code blocks can limit the *scope* of a variable, that is, the parts of a listing in which a specific variable is in effect. Two different code blocks may have no access whatsoever into one another's variable space.

Python doesn't treat curly brackets the way Java or C# do. Instead, the language uses whitespace (i.e., blank characters or indentation) when denoting code blocks. In Python, curly brackets are reserved for defining a dictionary or a set data type.

# First Adventures in Java

Now, in Listing 2-3, we had a program in Python where the user was asked for a number. The program then showed a comment on screen based on this input. Let's examine how Java deals with the same ordeal. It's somewhat more complicated, but fear not. We'll break it down afterward.

*Listing 2-4.* *A simple listing in Java demonstrating user keyboard input*

```java
import java.util.Scanner;

public class HappyProgram {
    public static void main(String args[]) {

        Scanner input_a = new Scanner(System.in);
        System.out.print("Enter a number: ");
        int YourNumber = input_a.nextInt();

if (YourNumber > 10) System.out.println("Your number is greater than ten") ;
if (YourNumber <= 10) System.out.println("Your number is ten or smaller") ;
    }
}
```

Compared to Python, Java does require more setting up. Programs written in Java can be extended using so-called Java Packages; these are basically data containers which add new features and functions into your projects. The very first line in Listing 2-4 adds interactive functionality to any Java program and needs to be there when we require user input.

Listing 2-4 simply incorporates a Java Package called *java.util* into the program. From this package, we retrieve the scanner function, which is then used to read keyboard input. We'll go through some of the most commonly used Java Packages as we progress through the book.

Let's now break down the mechanics related to user input in Listing 2-4:

```java
Scanner input_a = new Scanner(System.in);
```

What happens here is we create a *scanner object* called *input_a*. We could've called this object *happy_object* or *pink_tutu*. However, it's best to stick to at least a somewhat logical naming scheme. Moving on, we encounter the following lines of code:

```
System.out.print("Enter a number: ");
    int YourNumber = input_a.nextInt();
```

In the preceding snippet, we display a message using Java's standard print function. Notice how different it is from Python. Next, an integer variable (i.e., a whole number) called *YourNumber* is initialized. This is then sent to a function called *nextInt( )*, which awaits user input, expecting a whole number. The aforementioned function is a part of the Java Package *java.util.Scanner* we imported on the first line of the listing.

---

You may have noticed the ample use of the semicolon (;) in Listing 2-4. Java does indeed expect one after each instruction. Also, the Java syntax requires parentheses around variable comparisons and with most functions. All of these conventions apply in C#, too.

---

## Once More with C#

Next we'll glance at the same listing; only this time, it's written in C# (see Listing 2-5). You'll find it somewhat similar to the one in Java, but there are a few key differences which will be discussed after.

**Listing 2-5.** *A listing in C# demonstrating user keyboard input*

```
using System;

public class HappyProgram
{
    public static void Main()
    {
    Console.WriteLine("Enter a number: ");
    int YourNumber = Convert.ToInt16(Console.ReadLine());

        if (YourNumber > 10) Console.WriteLine("Your number is greater than ten");
        if (YourNumber <= 10) Console.WriteLine("Your number is ten or smaller");
    }
}
```

The first line in Listing 2-5 (i.e., *using System;*) activates a specific *namespace*. Namespaces in C# are container elements which help you organize your code. For one, they help you save time. Without the System namespace, instead of *Console.WriteLine*, we would be typing *System.Console.WriteLine* every time we printed things on screen. One can also declare their own custom namespaces which is something we'll be doing later in the book. For now, it suffices that you're aware of them.

---

Most programming languages need specific declarative statements in the source code, which often need not be unique for each project. This is referred to as *boilerplate code*. For example, in Listing 2-4, the line *public static void main(String args[ ])* and, in Listing 2-5, *public static void Main( )* may be classified as boilerplate code on the Java and C# sides of things, respectively. We'll examine this concept more in later chapters.

---

Now, compared to Java, C# uses a different lexicon for many of its functions. For printing text on screen, we have *Console.Writeline*. For user input, we have *Console.ReadLine* as is demonstrated by the following line:

```
int YourNumber = Convert.ToInt16(Console.ReadLine());
```

What happens here is we initialize an integer variable, YourNumber, and pass that on to a conversion function *Convert*. We tell it to wait for user input and expect a *signed 16-bit integer value*. These are whole numbers with a range from -32,768 to 32,768. That's ample room for what our user is most likely going to input.

---

*Unsigned 16-bit integers* carry values between 0 and 65,536, meaning they can't store negative values. If we need to store really large numbers, we could opt to using *32-bit integers,* which also have their signed (-2,147,483,647 to 2,147,483,647) and unsigned (0 to 4,294,967,295) counterparts. For the purposes of this book, we'll stick firmly to the smaller numbers.

---

# On Classes and Object-Oriented Programming

You may have noticed the word *class* appears several times in our listings. This is a crucial concept in *object-oriented programming (OOP)*, a popular programming paradigm. All of the three languages featured in the book incorporate OOP to varying degrees.

Any real-world or abstract scenario can be elegantly expressed using OOP. The two fundamental building blocks in this approach are known as *classes* and *objects*. Simply put, a class defines a blueprint for objects. For example, you may be developing software about gardening and write a class called *Plant*. You could then summon individual instances, known as objects, using the Plant class to populate your virtual garden. The various individual flora you created this way would share characteristics and variables with each other as defined in their originating class. Changing parts of class Plant at a later date would affect all future objects belonging to the said class. You could also create subclasses of Plant to cater for all the various roses and tulips you plan to model (as well as a class for garden gnomes).

OOP offers many benefits to software developers. Among these are the reusability of code and development security through class encapsulation. There are many fascinating facets to object-oriented programming. We'll go much deeper into this paradigm later in the book.

# The Basics of Flow Control: Loops

Variables aside, we have a bunch of logical structures at our disposal for getting things done with our coding. These structures constitute what is known as *flow control*. When any program listing is typed in, it's read by the computer from top to bottom. Quite often, processing within this program is to be repeated numerous times. It therefore makes sense to have the capabilities for looping and conditional program flow in place.

Loops in programming may introduce you to the concept of *iteration*. Iteration is the process of repeating specific steps for a usually predetermined amount of times in order to obtain a desirable result. A repeating sequence of actions in the context of programming is referred to as a *loop*. There are many ways to create these loops, and it also depends on the language being used. See Table 2-6 for sample implementations of these structures.

**Table 2-6.** Examples of flow control in three languages

| "While-loop" in Java | "For-loop" in C# | "For-loop" in Python |
|---|---|---|
| // Let's initialize a variable | // This is a fascinating loop | # This is a fun loop |
| int i=3; | **for**(int i=0; i<3; i++) | **for** i in range(10): |
| **while** (i>0) { | { | print("Hello number",i) |
| System.out.println | Console.WriteLine("Hello!"); | |
| ("Three hellos"); | } | |
| --i; | | |
| } | | |

# The While-Loop

The first iteration method in Table 2-6 is the while-loop as demonstrated in Java. This approach executes actions until the condition in the while function is met. In our example, the loop runs while the variable *i* is greater than zero. Aside from differences in command syntax when it comes to printing text on screen, the while-loop in Table 2-6 is identical in both Java and C#.

# The For-Loop in Detail

The example in C# in Table 2-6 may seem somewhat complicated. The structure in question, the *for-loop*, is an ancient technique consisting of several elements which will now be discussed.

The head (i.e., the part starting with *for*) contains instructions as to how many times the body (i.e., the part surrounded by curly brackets) is to be executed. In our example, the head part reads as follows:

- Define an auxiliary numeric variable *i* and give *i* the value of zero (int i=0;).

- Execute the body part of the loop as long as variable *i* is less than three (i<3;) after which you resume the program.

- Add one (1) to the value of *i* (i++).

Again, aside from differences in command syntax (i.e., System.out.println vs. Console.WriteLine), the middle example in Table 2-6 is identical in both Java and C#.

# Looping in Python

You'll perhaps notice the glaring absence of semicolons and curly brackets in our Python loop. The line containing the print command is indeed included into the loop's code block using indentation only. Also, instead of the somewhat more complicated structure of Java and C#, for-loops in Python can simply use a nifty function called *range* to set the number of iterations.

---

Sometimes we need to document changes to our code. Although pen and paper are fine, it's a better idea to do this inside a listing. To add lines that are not parsed by the computer, we can inject our listings with special characters. With Java and C#, we use two forward slashes, and for Python, we go with a hash mark, as was evident in Listing 2-5.

---

# In Closing

Finishing this chapter, you'll have hopefully gained understanding of the following:

- The main differences between interpreted and compiled programming languages

- What variables are in the context of programming and how to manipulate them

- How to define and manipulate variables and print text on screen using Java, C#, and Python

- Which are the six universal variable comparison operators

- What are the two fundamental concepts in object-oriented programming (OOP)

- The basics of programmatic flow control, including the if-statement and for-loops

In Chapter 3, we'll go beyond online compilers and set you up with some fine downloadable software as well as deepening your understanding of the concepts presented in this chapter. We'll be covering Windows, macOS, and Linux when it comes to software development environments.

# Setting Up Your Programming Environments

This chapter is dedicated to introducing you to the joys of *integrated development environments*. While online programming environments are fine for your first few listings, you really benefit from having some dedicated coding software on your own computer. Luckily there are a plethora of free IDEs available for your downloading pleasure. We'll cover this variety of software for the three most popular operating systems of 2021. But first, we'll address another fundamental concept: *computing architecture*.

## On Computing Architecture

A *clock cycle* represents a single action executed within a CPU. During each clock cycle, CPUs perform basic internal operations which form parts of any bigger tasks within your computer's ecosystem. Now, *clock speed* refers to the amount of clock cycles per second a CPU can muster and is usually denoted with the unit of *gigahertz (Ghz)*. For example, a 2.1 Ghz CPU offers 2.1 billion clock cycles per second. The more clock cycles per second a CPU offers, the faster a system will crunch its numbers.

© Robert Ciesla 2021

R. Ciesla, *Programming Basics*, https://doi.org/10.1007/978-1-4842-7286-2_3

Now, the term *computing architecture* is used to describe how much data a CPU can process per clock cycle. There are basically two major computing architectures in the current market: 32 and 64 bit. The latter is fast becoming the de facto architecture for most varieties of computing. Software written for 64-bit architecture makes better use of system resources, such as RAM, while also usually executing faster than its 32-bit counterparts.

Architecture implementation takes place in both hardware and software. Only 64-bit CPUs can run a 64-bit operating system, while still offering compatibility with older, 32-bit software (and operating systems). However, a 64-bit OS cannot usually be even installed on a computer with a 32-bit CPU.

As of the early 2000s, CPUs with support for 64-bit computing became increasingly popular. Unless you are using a truly ancient PC, chances are you're all set for 64-bit computing at least on the hardware side of things. See Table 3-1 for a rundown on these two architectures.

Big business is in the process of abandoning 32-bit technology altogether. In fact, starting with *macOS Catalina (10.15)*, Apple dropped support for 32-bit software completely. Microsoft, too, is leaving the world of 32 bits behind. As of May 2020, any ready-made computers will only be shipped with the 64-bit editions of *Windows 10*. Out of the big three operating systems, only some distributions of *Linux* still cater extensively for 32-bit hardware.

**Table 3-1.** A comparison of 32- and 64-bit computing architectures

|  | 32-bit architecture | 64-bit architecture |
|---|---|---|
| Features | Runs only 32-bit editions of operating systems, can run most legacy 16-bit software | Runs both 32- and 64-bit operating systems, typically does not support 16-bit software |
| Theoretical maximum RAM per system | 4 gigabytes (GB) or 4,294,967,296 bytes | 17,1 billion gigabytes (GB) or 18,446,744,073,709,551,616 bytes |
| Typical RAM amount in a system | Between 1 and 4 GB | Between 8 and 32 GB |

For the purposes of this book, you are not required to run any 64-bit software; a 32-bit operating system is just fine. However, in order to future-proof your devices, you should consider migrating to 64-bit operating systems as soon as you can.

# Bit-Derived Units Explained

Like you probably know by now, the smallest unit in computing is the bit. As with other quantities, it's impractical to measure things solely with the atomic unit. Therefore, we have bytes, megabytes, and gigabytes, to name just three (see Table 3-2).

Metric units (i.e., units using multipliers of power of ten) worked fine for the early days of personal computing. However, using these multipliers wasn't entirely accurate. For example, a 1 kilobyte file is actually 1024 bytes and not 1000 ($10^3$) as per the metric system.

A typical hard drive with the stated capacity of, say, 250 GB (i.e., 250,000,000,000 bytes) is actually 232.8 GB in size. Hardware manufacturers don't usually mention these things. Figure you may go.

In 1998, the *International Electrotechnical Commission (IEC)* created a more accurate measurement scheme. The new system used power-of-two multipliers. For example, a kilobyte became a *kibibyte* of 1024 bytes in size ($2^{10} = 1024$). These new units were sorely needed because they are much more accurate for measuring larger data pools.

**Table 3-2.** A comparison of the most commonly used metric and IEC-based data storage units

| Metric unit | Value (metric) | IEC unit | Value (IEC) |
|---|---|---|---|
| Bit (b) | 0 or 1 (atomic/smallest unit) | | |
| Byte (B) | Eight bits | | |
| Kilobyte (kB) | 1,000 bytes | Kibibyte (KiB) | 1024 bytes |
| Megabyte (MB) | 1,000,000 bytes | Mebibyte (MiB) | 1,048,576 bytes (1024 kibibytes) |
| Gigabyte (GB) | 1,000,000,000 bytes (one billion bytes) | Gibibyte (GiB) | 1,073,741,824 bytes (1024 mebibytes) |
| Terabyte (TB) | 1,000,000,000,000 bytes (one trillion bytes) | Tebibyte (TiB) | 1,099,511,627,776 bytes (1024 gibibytes) |

## Multitasking in 64 Bits

One of the major benefits of 64-bit computing is the greatly improved *multitasking* when compared to older 32-bit architecture. Multitasking refers to running several programs simultaneously. A typical programmer might have a great big IDE, *Photoshop*, *Spotify*, and 50 tabs open in *Firefox* at the same time on their computer. Having numerous gigabytes of RAM installed does away with a lot of the stutter and slowdown usually associated with scenarios involving running multiple programs. RAM upgrades are perhaps the most common way to push one's PC into higher performance.

## Identifying Your Operating System Architecture

You may want to check whether your operating system is 32 or 64 bits in its architecture. It's quick and easy.

- In Windows 10, go to *Settings* ➤ *System* ➤ *About*. You'll see the necessary details on this page.

- In Linux, open a terminal window and type *arch* and press enter to reveal your system architecture. An output displaying *x86_64* means you have a 64-bit edition of Linux. An output of *i386* or *i686* is displayed for 32-bit editions of this OS.

- As for *macOS,* every version of this operating system has been 64 bits (with varying degrees of backward compatibility for 32-bit software) since *Snow Leopard (10.6)* from 2009.

## Installing Eclipse for Java Development

Good development environments provide search features, syntax highlighting, and in some cases support for multiple programming languages. We'll first set you up with an environment specially made for Java development, the mighty *Eclipse IDE* by the Eclipse Foundation (see Figure 3-1).

---

*The Eclipse Project* was originally created by IBM in November 2001. *The Eclipse Foundation* then emerged in 2004 as an independent not-for-profit corporation. It was created as an open and transparent community around Eclipse.

---

Eclipse is available for *Windows, macOS,* and *Linux.* Visit the download page provided in the following, and simply click the link which reflects the type of operating system you're running. However, there is one caveat. The newest versions of Eclipse are only available for 64-bit editions of modern operating systems. In case you're still rocking a 32-bit OS, see a dedicated link for an older version of Eclipse. They too will suit our purposes just fine.

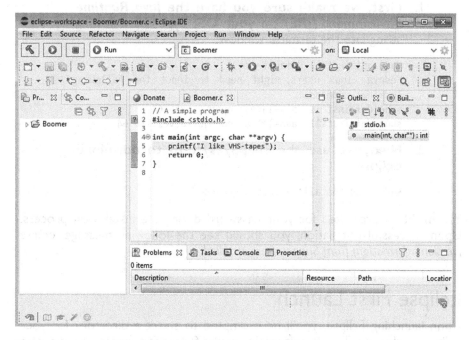

**Figure 3-1.** Eclipse in action

- **Download and install *Eclipse for Java Developers* (64-bit edition):** www.eclipse.org/downloads/packages/release/2020-12/r/eclipse-ide-java-developers

- **Download *Eclipse for Java Developers* (32-bit edition):** www.eclipse.org/downloads/packages/release/helios/sr1/eclipse-ide-java-developers

# Installing Eclipse for Linux

The Linux Repository may host an outdated version of Eclipse. For the installation of the most current version in Linux, we'll use the Snapcraft method offered by Canonical Ltd. This approach should work on all major distributions of Linux. Open a terminal window, and enter the following lines:

1. **First, we make sure you have the *Java Runtime Environment (JRE)* on your OS.** Type the following string into the terminal window:

   ```
   sudo apt install default-jre
   Fedora Linux users might need to input the following
   Terminal-commands:
   sudo dnf install java-latest-openjdk.x86_64
   sudo dnf install java-latest-openjdk-devel.x86_64
   ```

2. **Next, we use the snappy system to download Eclipse:**

   ```
   sudo snap install --classic eclipse
   ```

You might be prompted for your password during the installation process. Upon successful installation, you should see the following message: *eclipse (version information) from Snapcrafters installed.*

# Eclipse First Launch

Upon launching Eclipse, you'll be prompted to select a directory for your Eclipse workspace. The default setting works for most purposes. Let's create a new project. This is done by navigating to *File* ➤ *New* ➤ *Java Project* from the top menu bar. Next, you should see a window which awaits your project tile. Enter one and click *Create*.

A window will appear asking whether you want *module-info.java* to be created or not. This file is a *module declaration* used by the modular functionality of Java. For simple applications, it's fine if you choose *Don't Create*.

You will be taken to the main project view in Eclipse. We don't quite have a functional Java application on our hands yet. Now, on the left, you'll see the *Project Explorer*. Left-click your project name. Select *File* ➤ *New* ➤ *Class* from the top menu. Enter a name for this new class; it doesn't have to share your project's name.

Next, make absolutely sure you have ticked the box next to *public static void main(String args)*. This gives your project a *Java main method*. Without it, you can't execute your project. Finally, click *Finish* to go to your brand new Java code listing. You can now start coding under the main method.

# Great IDEs for C# Development

Let's now review some choices for your go-to C# needs. We'll start off with Microsoft's *Visual Studio* which is a popular multi-platform IDE chock full of great features, including on-the-fly error underlining. The software is available for Windows and macOS.

# Setting Up Visual Studio for Windows and Mac

Let's start with Visual Studio installation for Windows and macOS. First, you need to download the correct installer for the completely free Community Edition. This is a robust IDE for multiple languages, including C#.

- **Download *Visual Studio Community Edition*:**
  `https://visualstudio.microsoft.com/`
  `free-developer-offers/`

Upon launching the Visual Studio installer, you'll be eventually taken to a screen about *Workloads*. These basically refer to different scenarios of implementation for the various languages on offer in Visual Studio. You'll see four categories of Workloads for C# and other languages; they are *Web & Cloud, Desktop & Mobile, Gaming,* and *Other Toolsets* (see Figure 3-2). For our coding needs, let's tick the check box next to *.NET desktop development*. This will set us up with C# nicely.

Finally, click *Install* on the bottom right corner of the window. You may also choose to either install while downloading or to first download all necessary files and start the installation process afterward.

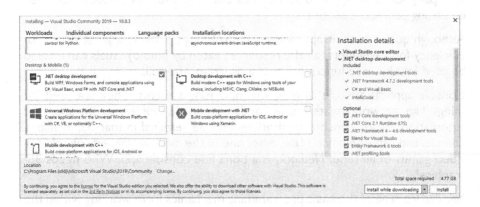

**Figure 3-2.** The installation screen for Microsoft's Visual Studio Community Edition

The first *.NET* was a software framework created by Microsoft in 2002 and released under a proprietary license. It offered streamlined development for C#, C++, and other popular languages. The framework received a major overhaul in 2016 under the name of *.NET Core.* This time it came out as open source and cross-platform by including support for macOS (and, to an extent, Linux). Microsoft has since deprecated the new version's name back to .NET.

# Starting a New Project in Visual Studio

After a potentially lengthy installation process, Visual Studio presents you with the option of signing in to a developer account (or registering one) for additional benefits. Feel free to skip this step. Next, you are to choose a color scheme for the IDE and click *Start Visual Studio.*

A few moments later, you'll arrive at the Visual Studio main window. When you click *Create New Project*, you are presented with a variety of programming templates, including those specifically for C#. For our needs, the *Console App* is appropriate. After a moment or two, Visual Studio will have created your project files, and you can start coding underneath the main function.

# Console vs. GUI Applications

There is a universal distinction between so-called console applications and those with a graphical user interface (GUI). The former are presented using a bare-bones text-based interface, while the latter provide their users with more visuals and, in general, additional input methods (such as a mouse or trackpad). Console apps do sometimes utilize text-based *pseudographics* for emulating geometric shapes.

Although quaint in their appearance, console apps provide a great degree of efficiency for developers; all the resources eaten by (audio)visuals can instead be used for the core functionality of a program, after all.

Console applications are all over our operating systems. They are used for things like network-related tasks and, potentially, numerous instances of automation. Major console applications include *Terminal* in macOS, *Windows Console*, and *Linux Command Line*. Also, one of the most acclaimed role-playing video games of all time, *Nethack,* is a bona fide console app. Who needs 3D graphics?

You can learn all of the basic programming mechanics from working within the realm of console apps. Although we'll touch on GUI-based development, the focus of this book is mostly in the text-based environment.

# C# in Linux: Introducing MonoDevelop

As of Q1 2021, Visual Studio is not available for Linux. However, *MonoDevelop* provides everything you need to get started coding C# within a flexible IDE.

- **Follow these instructions on the MonoDevelop site:** `www.monodevelop.com/download`

Navigate to the Mono repository closest to the Linux distribution and version you are currently using from the preceding download page (e.g., Debian). Next, you will be copy-pasting a lot of commands into your terminal window. You may need to wait several minutes for the installation to complete depending on your hardware. Afterward, MonoDevelop should reside safely in your Applications folder.

Open MonoDevelop by clicking its icon. Navigate to *File ➤ New Solution*. A new window will open. Click *.NET* under *Other*, and select *Console Project*. Finally, click *Next* on the bottom right corner. Another window will open prompting you for a project name. Enter anything you feel is suitable, and click *Create*.

You should next arrive at a listing for a generic hello world application in C#. Either navigate to *Run ➤ Start Without Debugging* or click the play icon on the top left part of the MonoDevelop IDE to execute the listing.

---

You might have to execute the following additional lines in the terminal window if you are prompted by an error ending with "cannot find the specified file" after trying to run/debug a program in MonoDevelop:

```
cd /usr/lib
sudo mkdir gnome-terminal
cd gnome-terminal
sudo ln -s /usr/libexec/gnome-terminal-server
```

---

You're now all set to develop some dandy console applications for Linux.

# PyCharm for Python Development

When it comes to development with Python, there's one piece of software which stands above the rest. *PyCharm* is a multi-platform IDE with excellent features like intelligent code completion. The suite is available in both paid and free editions; we'll be working with the latter. The following link will direct you to the version of PyCharm your OS supports.

- **Download *PyCharm Community Edition***: *www.jetbrains.com/pycharm/download*

PyCharm's installation process for both Windows and macOS is quite straightforward. For the former, run the executable you downloaded and follow the onscreen instructions. With macOS, just double-click the image file (ending in .dmg), and drag the PyCharm icon into your Applications folder.

---

When installing PyCharm on Windows, you might be presented with a password prompt even when you are on an account without password protection. Simply click cancel to continue with the installation.

---

To begin experimenting with PyCharm, click *Create Project*. You'll then be given the opportunity to name your project as well as to choose some other options for it. The project name doubles as the directory location for all of your PyCharm-project files. When you've settled for an appropriate title, click *Create* on the bottom right of the window.

---

To make starting out easier, PyCharm gives you the option of creating a welcome script for you. It's best to enable this option. Make sure the box is ticked next to *Create a main.py welcome script* when making a new project.

---

PyCharm might download some additional components the first time you create a new project. Installation of these components might take a while. When your new project files are ready, you'll be taken into the main coding view in PyCharm. You are now free to edit the file *main.py* and experiment with this amazing IDE for Python.

The file *main.py* will be populated with some Python code upon first opening your new project. You can erase all of it and type your own code in its place.

# Installing PyCharm for Linux

The best way to get PyCharm running on your Linux is to use snap packages. Simply open a terminal window, and feed it the following line:

```
sudo snap install pycharm-community --classic
```

# Software Vermin: Bugs

Have you ever ended up with your computer jammed and/or your text document(s) lost? Chances are you encountered a *software bug* in action. Bugs in the context of software mean glitches caused by a faulty program code; they can come in the form of typos by the programmer(s) or more commonly from some arcane design error. All those software updates for your operating system are basically there to fix bugs (and on occasion offer new features). See Table 3-3 for a rundown on the most common software bugs and issues.

**Table 3-3.** The most common categories of software issues/bugs

| Software bug | Examples | Software issue | Examples |
| --- | --- | --- | --- |
| Syntactic | Incorrect use of language syntax, e.g., using wrong variable comparison operators | Interface | Lacking user interface functionality, e.g., missing navigation buttons or other critical elements |
| Arithmetic | Division by zero, variable range overflow | Security | Weak authentication, unnecessary exposure of critical system components |
| Logical | Poor program flow control, e.g., infinite or compromised loops | Communication | Lack of user documentation, poor labeling of user interface elements, unintuitive error prompts |
| Resources | Use of uninitialized variables, exhausting system RAM by not freeing unneeded variable space | Teamwork neglect | Illogical labeling of code elements/variables, poor commenting |

# On Debugging and Testing

*Debugging* is the art of discovering and fixing bugs found in software. A *debugger* provides software developers the tools to fix bugs as they happen and before they potentially wreak havoc on a user's computer. This is another feature of a solid IDE and naturally belongs in every solution presented in this chapter.

Debugging can range from simple error highlighting in the IDE editor to exhaustive data collection and analysis. A typical debugging component allows the programmer to examine the software being developed while it's running, line by line if necessary. Code-written high-level programming languages, like Java and Python, are typically easier to debug. Lower-level languages, like procedural C, leave more control to the programmer; this can lead to issues like memory corruption more frequently.

Heavy debugging is absolutely essential for larger software projects. For our needs, we needn't go very deep into this topic. At this point, it suffices you are aware of what the term means.

Debugging is related to the sometimes overlooked area of software development: *testing*. Although testing incorporates debugging, there's much more to it. A testing team is responsible for reporting whether the software product functions correctly under its intended usage scenarios. However, not even a large-scale testing process is expected to find every single flaw in a software project.

Software testing can be roughly split into *functional* and *nonfunctional* branches. The former focuses on comparing the functioning of software and its components against a set of specifications. Nonfunctional testing refers to issues related (but not limited) to performance, usability, and security. Localization, including development for non-Western markets, is also a part of nonfunctional software testing. Localization involves incorporating fluent and appropriate translated language with varying focus on cultural sensitivity.

The details of the testing process depend on the type of target audience. Video game developers, especially when it comes to the smaller teams, sometimes skimp on testing (much to their detriment). Essential software, such as that found in banking and finance, is expected to undergo the strictest levels of testing. Larger software projects require a highly organized team of testers. Due to economic reasons, testing for large-scale software is often outsourced to businesses abroad.

# Debugging: Essential Approaches

We shall now peek at some of the most common methods for debugging code in some detail:

- **Tracing/print debugging**: This method simply means paying close attention to the results of every executed line of code by printing them out on screen, one by one. Close attention can be paid to the contents of variables and other data structures as they're altered during a program's execution. Tracing is something that works great for smaller projects, such as the tutorials within this book.

- **Record and replay debugging**: With this approach, parts of a program's execution are recorded and played back to examine its potential shortcomings. This doesn't refer to the external or visual playback of software; rather it focuses on state-level proceedings within a program.

- **Post-mortem debugging**: This method consists of analyzing the post-crash log data on a program. Many types of software write log files on disk after serious malfunctions, including most operating systems. These files can then be examined for clues as to which bugs caused a crash.

- **Remote debugging**: Debugging doesn't have to take place on the device which runs the program of focus. Using popular networking methods, such as Wi-Fi or USB cabling, devices in different roles and form factors can be connected to work together. Doing it remotely is the most common approach when writing and debugging software for Android and iOS, as the development machine is almost always a separate full-sized computer.

- **Bug clustering**: This is a useful approach whenever a particularly large amount of bugs are found. The programmer first identifies any and all common characteristics in the bugs. The issues are then classified into specific groups which share their attributes, the logic being that even if a few bugs within a cluster are solved, the rest should follow.

- **Code simplification**: Sometimes the best strategy for eliminating bugs is to (more or less temporarily) remove portions of the functional code around them. This obviously works best for bugs of the more clandestine/ shy nature. When you are not yet sure of what doesn't work (i.e., what's causing a crash), remove the parts that obviously do, one by one, and lure the bug out.

# In Closing

Finishing this chapter, you'll have gained an understanding of the following:

- The main differences between 32-bit and 64-bit computing architectures and how to identify which variety your operating system is running on

- How the most common bit-derived data units are defined

- What an *integrated development environment (IDE)* refers to and how to get one for your operating system

- The core differences between *console applications* and applications utilizing a *graphical user interface (GUI)*

- The most common types of software bugs/issues

- What debugging and software testing refer to

The next chapter is dedicated to the wonders of object-oriented programming (OOP) in detail. As touched on in Chapter 2, this is a very important paradigm every budding coder should be able to work with.

# Object-Oriented Programming (OOP)

This chapter is all about object-oriented programming in detail. This monumental paradigm changed the world of programming and has since become somewhat of a de facto approach in software design. We'll next go through many of the concepts crucial to the object-oriented paradigm. During this chapter, we'll present concepts related to OOP mostly using the Java language for clarity, not completely forsaking C# and Python, of course.

## Procedural vs. Object-Oriented Paradigms

As mentioned in Chapter 2, there are currently basically two major programming paradigms: procedural and object oriented. The late 1970s were an exciting time in computer science. Prior to that, most of programming was done strictly in the realm of procedural languages, which operates under a so-called "top-down" design paradigm. Basically, with this approach, the programmer takes care of the details last. Most focus goes into the main function of the program.

© Robert Ciesla 2021

R. Ciesla, *Programming Basics*, https://doi.org/10.1007/978-1-4842-7286-2_4

The object-oriented revolution was kicked off by the release of C++. Released in 1985, the language quickly became widely adopted for most purposes. Using a "bottom-up" design approach, C++ and other object-oriented languages focus on defining the data first which is often modeled after real-life phenomena. In addition, they provide plenty of additional functionality compared to their procedural counterparts. This includes *encapsulation*, a technique which is used to isolate parts of the code from one and other by implementing access specifiers. We'll look at encapsulation and other object-oriented specifics in more detail next.

See Table 4-1 for the main differences between procedural and object-oriented programming languages.

**Table 4-1.** The main differences between the two main programming paradigms

|  | Procedural programming | Object-oriented programming |
|---|---|---|
| Example languages | (Procedural) C, Pascal, BASIC | C#, C++, Java, Python |
| Based on | The abstract world | Real-world scenarios |
| Approach | Top down: the main problem is broken down into sub-procedures | Bottom up: data classes are created first |
| Emphasis | Functions (i.e., procedures) | Data (i.e., classes) |
| Inheritance | Not supported | Supported |
| Encapsulation (data security) | Low: no access modifiers | High: multiple levels of access modifiers |
| Method overloading (multiple methods with the same name) | Not supported | Supported |

# Classes, Inheritance, and UML

Let's revisit the most fundamental concepts of object-oriented programming (OOP) as we only touched on some of those in Chapter 2. We'll continue with the concepts of *classes* and *objects*. By now you may know that in OOP, a class is a kind of blueprint for creating code objects.

Now, with larger software projects especially, it's often a good idea to put pen to paper, so to speak, before writing a line of code. One of the best and most popular tools for visualizing object-oriented software is to use *Universal Modeling Language (UML)*. Created by *Rational Software* in the mid-1990s, UML has since become a ubiquitous tool in software engineering. Let's sample some with a *class diagram* about ice cream (see Figure 4-1).

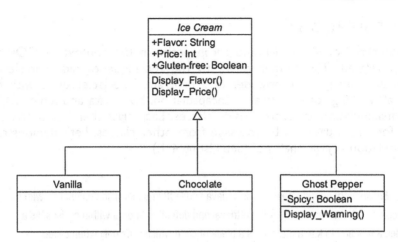

**Figure 4-1.** A simple class diagram demonstrating the basics of UML

The topmost box in Figure 4-1 (i.e., *Ice Cream*) is an *abstract class*. Basically, these are classes which cannot be used to create objects with. Why have them then? Well, abstract classes can hold the same type of information as regular classes. They can have subclasses, too. The purpose of an abstract class is to provide some shared information for its subclasses to inherit and create objects with. In many cases, their use simplifies the design process.

The three boxes below our abstract class are known as *subclasses*. They demonstrate *inheritance*, a crucial concept in OOP. *Vanilla, Chocolate,* and *Ghost Pepper* receive all the variables and methods which their *superclass*, Ice Cream, has built in. Pay attention to how the boxes are connected. Different varieties of arrows describe different things in UML. An empty arrowhead, as shown in Figure 4-1, connotes simple inheritance. In UML, one must also pay attention to the direction of the arrow(s).

Now, you denote abstract classes in UML by italicizing their name; regular classes are not generally stylized in any way. Next, a class box lists its variables and their data types. A plus (+) before a variable denotes that it's public, while a minus (-) refers to a private variable. Finally, we list any methods found in our classes, like we did with *Display_Flavor( )* and all the others in Figure 4-1.

---

There's more to UML than the elements we've introduced so far. We'll go into much more detail with this incredible modeling language in later chapters of the book. For now, it suffices you understand how UML can help you visualize a software project.

---

# Encapsulation

The concepts of *abstraction* and *encapsulation* in the context of OOP are closely related. The former refers to the technique of hiding irrelevant information from the user/coder of a program. The latter deals with the internal workings of software; in encapsulation, both data and functions for their manipulation are stored inside classes. Each class then has controls in place for which data can be accessed from other classes. Let's demonstrate encapsulation in Java, shall we? (See Listing 4-1.)

---

*Get* and *Set* are very important keywords in Java and OOP in general. In conjunction with the *return* command, they are used for the retrieval and definition of data within classes. As a reminder, a function (a.k.a. a method) is a piece of code which runs only when called.

---

**Listing 4-1.** *A class definition in Java with Get- and Set-functions (file name Geezer.java)*

```java
public class Geezer {
  // The private-access modifier is used to limit access from other classes
  private String name;

  // The Get-function is used to retrieve name variable
  // Its naming convention is non-capitalized "get" and capitalized variable
  public String getName() {
    return name;
  }

  // The Set-function defines data
  public void setName(String newName) {
    this.name = newName;
  }
}
```

---

Listing 4-1 cannot be executed in IDEs or online development environments as it lacks the Java main method. The listing is provided for demonstrative purposes only. We'll move into actually executable Java code shortly.

---

We start out our class definition by giving it a name, which is also to be its file name. In our example, it shall be *Geezer*. The first thing we do with it is to define a variable of the type *String* (obviously for storing geezers' names). The keyword *private* before the variable definition is known as an *access modifier*.

Private methods and variables can only be accessed within the class they are defined in (in our case only from within Geezer).

The getName method uses the return keyword to retrieve a geezer's name. The method is created both public and of the value String. This is simply because it's expected to return the value of a String variable.

Let's next break down the setName method we defined in Listing 4-1. The keyword pair *public void* specifies a method which doesn't return a value. It goes well with set functions in general since they are used to define variables and not to retrieve values from them. The keyword *this* in Java simply addresses the object containing the method.

# Your (Potentially) First Java Object

Classes are great for organizing data, but they can do much more. Using the geezer class as a starting point, let's add code to create an actual object in Java (see Listing 4-2).

**Listing 4-2.** *A class definition with a main method in Java (file name Geezer.java)*

```java
public class Geezer {
  private String name;

  public String getName() {
    return name;
  }

  public void setName(String newName) {
    this.name = newName;
  }
    // We add a main-method so we can actually experiment with our class
    public static void main(String args[]) {
    // Next we create an object using the geezer-class as a blueprint
    // We'll call our object "some_geezer"
    // and use Java's built-in new-method to bring it to life
    Geezer some_geezer = new Geezer();
    // Next we invoke the setName-method to give our geezer a name
    some_geezer.setName("John");
    // Finally we access our geezer-object to print out a name
    // in two different ways
    System.out.println("Hello, my name is "+some_geezer.name+" the geezer!");
    System.out.println("Can you repeat that? "+"It's "+some_geezer.getName());
    }
}
```

In Listing 4-2, we use both a so-called dot operator (i.e., *some_geezer.name*) and the getName method to read data from our object. The dot operator is also called the *member operator.*

---

The line *public static void main(String[ ] args)* is where each Java program begins its processing, and things start appearing on screen for the user. The part stating *String[] args* basically means that the program accepts a single string of text as its input from whoever executes it (e.g., a user might start a program by typing in "myProgram hello" instead of "myProgram," potentially for various effects).

---

# Java Alphabet Soup: JDK, JVM, and JRE

Before continuing with OOP, let's take a gander at the three of the most crucial software components for Java development. There's no doubt you'll come across these terms rather frequently during your programming adventures. First, there's the *Java Development Kit (JDK)*. This is the central core collection of classes and tools needed to code in Java. The JDK comes in several varieties.

Next, we have the *Java Runtime Environment (JRE)*. This component is used to combine the code output done inside the JDK with some additional required software libraries, allowing Java programs to actually execute.

Finally, we have the *Java Virtual Machine (JVM)*. A Java program created on a desktop PC can run on any device that has JVM installed. This approach of running Java on a dedicated virtual machine therefore creates a great degree of platform independence.

---

As you may remember from Chapter 2, Java is an *interpreted language*. When executing a program written in Java, the compiler generates *bytecode*. This is an intermediate format which needs the Java Virtual Machine (JVM) to run; you cannot start a bytecode program without it. As the JVM is available for most modern computers and devices, this approach makes Java almost universally platform independent.

---

# Objects in C#

Having created our (potentially) first object in Java, let's now do the same in C#. See Listing 4-3, which has exactly the same functionality as Listing 4-2. This will demonstrate the many similarities in syntax which Java and C# share.

*Listing 4-3.* A class definition with a main method in C# (file name Geezer.cs)

```
using System;

public class Geezer {
  private String name;

  public String getName() {
    return name;
  }

  public void setName(String newName) {
    this.name = newName;
  }

public static void Main(string[] args) {
    Geezer some_geezer = new Geezer();
    some_geezer.setName("John");
    // The next two lines differ the most between our Java and C# listings
    Console.WriteLine("Hello, my name is "+some_geezer.name+" the geezer!");
    Console.WriteLine("Can you repeat that? "+"It's "+some_geezer.getName());
    }
}
```

# Static and Public Methods in Java and OOP

We'll now delve deeper into writing various kinds of methods. There are basically two varieties of methods in OOP: *static* and *public*. We already experimented with the latter in Listings 4-2 and 4-3.

---

**Note** A method can actually use both qualifiers, as is the case with the famous Java main method, *public static void main( )*.

---

Now, the main difference between the two varieties is that static methods don't need to be summoned using an object; you can call them without any specific instances of a class. However, static methods can't use class variables as demonstrated in Listing 4-4.

*Listing 4-4.* A class definition with a main method in Java (HappyMethods.java)

```
public class HappyMethods {
private int x=10, y=10;

  // A static method can't use our class variables
  static void myStaticMethod() {
```

```java
    System.out.println("Hello! I'm a static method and I can't use x or y.");
    // System.out.println(x + " + " + y + " = " + (x+y));
    // The line above would return an error
  }

  // A public method can use our class variables for some rudimentary
     arithmetic
  public void myPublicMethod() {
    System.out.println(x + " + " + y + " = " + (x+y));
  }

  // Our main method
  public static void main(String[] args) {
    myStaticMethod(); // Call the static method
    HappyMethods myObj = new HappyMethods(); // Create an object of HappyMethods
    myObj.myPublicMethod(); // Call the object's public method
  }
}
```

# Constructor Methods

An object receives initial values for all of its variables from the class definition. However, whenever an object is created, a constructor can be called to set all or parts of this variable data instead.

You can create new constructors simply by defining methods which accept extra attributes. These attributes are then passed on to each object, as needed, to replace the original values defined in the class. See Listing 4-5 for an example.

---

A constructor method <u>must</u> have an identical name with the class it's included in. In our example program, the two constructors are both titled *Movie* as per their originating class.

---

**Listing 4-5.** *A listing in Java demonstrating the use of constructor methods (Movie.java)*

```java
public class Movie {
  // Class variables and their default values
  private String title="Jack and Jill";
  private int release_year = 2011;

  // This is a default constructor. Java creates them automatically if need be
  public Movie() {
  }
```

```
// This is a constructor-method for setting both movie title and release year
public Movie(String name, int year) {
  release_year = year;
  title = name;
}
// This is a constructor for setting the movie title only
public Movie(String name) {
  release_year = 2021;
  title = name;
}

public static void main(String[] args) {
  // Create three objects based on class "Movie"
  Movie myMovie = new Movie("Jack and Jill 2");
  Movie myMovie2 = new Movie("The Ridiculous 6", 2015);
  Movie myMovie3 = new Movie();
  // Display the data stored in these three objects
  System.out.println(myMovie.title + " (" + myMovie.release_year+")");
  System.out.println(myMovie2.title + " (" + myMovie2.release_year+")");
  System.out.println(myMovie3.title + " (" + myMovie3.release_year+")");
  }
}
```

Now, in Listing 4-5, we summon three objects all based on the class *Movie*. All of these objects use different constructor methods to bring them to life.

The first object, dealing with the theoretical (but assuredly wonderful) movie *Jack and Jill 2*, is created using the constructor method which accepts a single string. The second object in Listing 4-5 uses the more versatile constructor which accepts both a string and an integer. The third and final object in our example is created using the most basic constructor available, which accepts no attributes whatsoever; it will assign the default values ("Jack and Jill" and 2011) into our object, as entered into the class definition.

# Overloading Methods

In OOP, you can have multiple methods of the same name without an issue, as long as the quantity and data type of their parameters are different (see Listing 4-6).

*Listing 4-6.* *A listing in Java demonstrating the overloading of methods (OverloadingFun.java)*

```java
public class OverloadingFun {

// Method for returning a middle-initial as an integer
static int MakeName(int middle) {
  return middle;
}

// Method for combining three strings into a full name
static String MakeName(String first, String mid, String last) {
  return first + mid + last;
}
public static void main(String[] args) {

  // Define an integer using our first method
  int integer_initial = MakeName(80); // 80 stands for 'P' in the ASCII-system

  // Convert this integer into single character-type using typecasting
  char middle_initial=(char)integer_initial;

  // Convert the new character variable into a string
  String mid=String.valueOf(middle_initial);

  // Add all three names to create full name using the second method
  String fullname = MakeName("Rick ", mid, " Astley");

  System.out.println("Full name: " + fullname);
}
}
```

Listing 4-6 features two methods called *MakeName*. The first method accepts integer values, while its sibling takes three strings. In order for the latter to do its job, the aforementioned integer value is first converted into a single character variable. This is done using Java's *typecasting* functionality and results in the letter "P" being stored into the variable *integer_initial*. This variable is then converted into a string using Java's *valueOf*-function.

Finally, we combine three strings, including the middle initial, into the name of a popular British pop singer.

# Access Modifiers in More Detail

By now, you have encountered access modifiers several times in our listings. Let's recap them next; they are very crucial in OOP, after all. Also, there's more to them than *private* or *public*. See Tables 4-2 and 4-3 for rundowns on the most common access modifiers in Java and C#, respectively. You will notice both languages have a different number of access modifiers, although they both basically adhere to the same OOP logic. Also, classes can have access to packages in Java.

**Table 4-2.** The most common access modifiers in Java

| Access modifier | When used with | Accessibility |
|---|---|---|
| *public* | Classes | Accessible by other classes |
| *protected* | | Accessible by the declaring and derived classes, and classes in the same package |
| *final* | | Class cannot inherited by any others |
| *abstract* | | Class is abstract; it cannot instantiate objects |
| *public* | Variables, methods, constructors | Code is accessible by all classes |
| *private* | | Code is only accessible by the declared class |
| *default (i.e., none specified)* | | Code is only accessible in the same package |
| *final* | | Variables and methods can't be modified |

As a reminder, in Java, a *package* refers to a group of related classes. We use the *import* keyword in our program listings to bring specific classes (e.g., *import package.name.happyclass*) or full packages (e.g., *import package.name.\**) into our projects for additional functionality. The asterisk character (*) used in the latter type of imports is called a *wildcard*.

# Why Access Modifiers Matter

You may be wondering what specific uses access modifiers actually offer; now would be a good time to review some scenarios in which they provide definite benefits. One such scenario involves teamwork. Encapsulated data protects especially larger projects against human errors. With encapsulated code programmers need not necessarily know *how* a method works; what matters is the output. This often speeds up development time.

Also, the correct use of access modifiers makes programs more readable from the programmer's point of view in general. Updating and maintaining encapsulated software projects is usually more straightforward than those of the procedural (i.e., non-OOP) kind.

---

Remember, encapsulation in OOP covers two meanings. First, it's a term used to describe the approach of pairing data with methods using classes. Second, it refers to restricting direct access to data on the programming level using access modifiers.

---

# The C# Assembly and Access Modifiers

Before we get to the slightly different landscape of C# access modifiers, let's review an important and related concept. An *assembly* in C# refers to the output of your project, as in a user-executable file usually with the file extension of .exe in the Windows environment (e.g., *happyprogram.exe*). It is the smallest unit of deployment in the language. Assemblies usually contain other resources used by a program, including image data. They also host your project metadata, such as its version information, and potentially a list of which other assemblies are needed to execute the program; larger projects may consist of numerous assemblies.

Now, let's review the six C# access modifiers. They may seem quite interchangeable right now, but by the time you finish this book, you'll have gotten familiar with them all with an understanding of how they're all needed (see Table 4-3).

**Table 4-3.** The six access modifiers of C#

| Access modifier | Accessibility |
| --- | --- |
| *Public* | Accessible by all other classes |
| *Private* | Only accessible from within the declared class |
| *Protected* | Accessible from within the declaring class and from within any class derived from this declaring class |
| *Internal* | Access is limited to classes defined within the current assembly |
| *protected internal* | Access is limited to classes defined within the current assembly AND/OR classes derived from them residing in other assemblies |
| *private protected* | Accessible from within the declaring class and from within any class derived from this declaring class, but only within the same assembly |

# Accessing Classes with C#

Let's get back to coding. Most of this chapter has used Java so far. Let's next create an original OOP listing for C# instead to demonstrate its take on access modifiers (see Listing 4-7).

**Listing 4-7.** *A C# listing demonstrating inheritance and the use of access modifiers*

```csharp
using System;
class Protected_Class {

    // Define a protected string variable, fruit
    protected String fruit;

    public Protected_Class()
    { fruit = "Noni fruit"; }
}

// Make a new derived class using the colon-operator
class Derived_Class : Protected_Class {

    // This method from Derived_Class can access Protected_Class
    public String getFruit()
    { return fruit; }
}

class Program {
    // Main execution begins below
    public static void Main(string[] args)
    {
            // Create two objects, one from each class
            Protected_Class Object1 = new Protected_Class();
            Derived_Class Object2 = new Derived_Class();
            // Display our string variable using a method from the derived
                class
            Console.WriteLine("Your favorite fruit is: {0}", Object2.
            getFruit());
    }
}
```

Listing 4-7 starts off with the creation of a class we'll call *Protected_Class* for clarity's sake. This class holds one constructor which sets a protected variable, *fruit*. A second class, *Derived_Class*, is created next and made to inherit the attributes of the first class using the colon (:) operator. Derived_Class may now access data from Protected_Class, even its protected variable. This can be done using a get method, so we'll make one just for this class and call it *getFruit( )*.

Next, we're moving on to the main method of Listing 4-7. Here, we create two objects, one from each class we defined earlier. Notice how the syntax for creating objects in C# is identical to the one Java uses.

The last line in our main method displays a message with the contents of the string variable; this is known as a *formatted string*. In C#, variables are displayed in text using curly brackets (C-derived languages really love them in general). The element {0} refers to the first (and, in this case, the only) variable we are going to display next to the message. If we had a second variable to print out in our string, we would do it with {1}—and so on.

## Once More, with UML

To further prepare you for the wonders of the Unified Modeling Language, let's turn Listing 4-7 into UML, shall we? Actually, there's more to this language than class diagrams; with UML, we can also visualize objects. In Figure 4-2, we have both the class (left) and object diagrams of Listing 4-7.

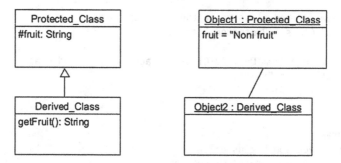

**Figure 4-2.** Class (left) and object diagrams of Listing 4-7 in UML

There's a couple of things you should take away from the rather straightforward Figure 4-2. First of all, protected members of a class are represented with the hashtag (#) symbol in front of them. In our example, this refers to the string-variable *fruit*. Also, object diagrams in UML use a specific format. The header has the object name, a colon operator (:) surrounded by spaces, and, finally, the name of the class this object is instantiated from. In addition, the header is fully underlined. In UML, object diagrams' variables are expected to display their contents; hence, we have the delicious "Noni fruit" in ours since that's what the constructor method of the class stated.

---

UML class diagrams represent a system as a whole, while object diagrams represent a system's detailed state at a specific point in time. Think of the former as a blueprint and the latter as a snapshot of a system in action.

---

# Protected Access: Java vs. C#

As close as Java and C# are in syntax and their logical approaches, there are some subtle differences which can be confusing at first. For example, the access modifier *protected* is treated differently between the two languages.

In Java, *protected* is equivalent to *protected internal* in C# as in it's accessible only by the declaring or derived class, or a class in the same *package* (in Java) or *assembly* (in C#).

As you may remember from Table 4-3, a bona fide *protected* modifier in C# is only accessible from within the declaring class and from within any class derived from the original class.

# Python and OOP

We have not forgotten about Python, and, yes, it's as object oriented as it gets. Although the language supports all major OOP techniques, the syntax is quite different to that of Java and C#. For one, most of those lovely curly brackets remain absent. Also, constructors in Python are defined with the keyword *__init__( )* (that's two underscores on each side).

---

In Python, whitespace becomes a very important factor. As mentioned in Chapter 2, indentation is an integral part of the Python syntax and is used to denote code blocks inside listings.

---

Now, let's make a simple class application in Python. In Listing 4-8, we create a class and a constructor method and also instantiate an object using the said class.

**Listing 4-8.** *A simple Python listing demonstrating OOP*

```
class Publisher:
          def __init__(self, name):
          self.name = name

"Create new object, cool_publisher, from the above class"
cool_publisher = Publisher("Apress")
"Display its name"
print(cool_publisher.name, "is cool!")
```

Gazing upon Listing 4-8, you'll immediately notice the differences to Java and C#. First off, the class *Publisher* consists of three separate code blocks, separated by three different levels of indentation. Python will actually throw out an error if this formatting logic isn't followed. Thankfully, most Python IDEs add whitespace automatically where applicable.

In Python, class and constructor declarations end with a colon (:). The expression *self* is used to address the classes' variables for each object it produces. Creating objects in Python is rather straightforward; we give them a name and assign a class with a constructor of our choosing. In Listing 4-8, there's only one constructor which accepts values for the publisher class's sole variable, *name*.

Let's next try something a little bit more complicated in Python (see Listing 4-9).

**Listing 4-9.** *A listing in Python demonstrating class construction*

```python
"Create and initialize a global variable"
potato_count = 0
class Potato:
    "Make a constructor"
    def __init__(self, *args):
        global potato_count # point out potato_count is indeed global
        "country defaults to Finland if no value is given"
        self.country = "Finland"
        "Take the first argument as diameter"
        self.diameter = args[0]
        "Take the second argument as cultivar"
        self.cultivar = args[1]
        "Increase global variable value by one"
        potato_count += 1

        "If over two arguments are given assume the third one is for country"
        if len(args) > 2:
            self.country = args[2]

    "Make a method for displaying object information"
    def printInfo(self):
        print("My cultivar is", self.cultivar, "and my diameter is", self.
        diameter, "inches")
        #If the country-variable is not empty (!= "") display it"
        if self.country != "":
            print("I was grown in", self.country)

"Create three objects of class Potato"
potato1 = Potato(3, "Lemin kirjava")
potato2 = Potato(5, "French Fingerling", "France", "This does nothing")

potato1.printInfo()
potato2.printInfo()
print("Total potato-cultivars listed:", potato_count)
```

The output of Listing 4-9 should look like this:

*My cultivar is Lemin kirjava and my diameter is 3 inches*

*I was grown in Finland*

*My cultivar is French Fingerling and my diameter is 5 inches*

*I was grown in France*

*Total potato-cultivars listed: 2*

Our slightly more complicated Python listing introduces several new concepts. One of those is *global variables*. These refer to variables which can be used at any point within a Python listing, both inside and outside of methods (of any class).

Next in Listing 4-9, we have the line *def __init__(self, *args):* which is the sole constructor for our Potato class. Instead of accepting specific data types, it takes a list of arguments as indicated by the expression *\*args*.

---

Python doesn't support method overloading per se, unlike Java and C#. If we were to enter any number of methods into a class for overloading purposes, each of these methods would simply override the previous one.

---

To assign an argument into a variable, we use *args[0]* for the first argument and *args[1]* for the second. As you can tell, Python begins counting arguments from zero.

Now, Python has a handy built-in function for determining the length of lists and other data structures, *len*. This is put to use in the following line in our listing *if len(args) > 2:* which simply means "if the length of arguments exceeds two." Basically our program accepts up to three arguments; the rest are simply discarded. This in turn is demonstrated with object *potato2* when we give it a total of four arguments; the last argument has no effect.

As for *potato_count*, our global variable, its value is increased by one every time a new object is instantiated from the Potato class. This naturally reflects the total number of Potato objects rather accurately.

# Inheritance in Python

Let's cover one more important topic before closing the chapter. Inheritance in Python is quite simple to implement (see Listing 4-10).

*Listing 4-10.* *A Python listing demonstrating inheritance. The child class definition is in bold*

```python
class Computer:
  def __init__(self, *args):
    self.type = args[0]
    self.cpu = args[1]
  "Define a method for displaying type"
  def printType(self):
    print("I use a", self.type, "as my daily driver.")

"Create a child class, Desktop"
class Desktop(Computer):
  def __init__(self, *args):
    Computer.__init__(self, *args)
    self.color = args[2]

"Create an object using Desktop-class"
computer1 = Desktop("Commodore 64", "MOS 8500", "beige")

computer1.printType()
print("It has a", computer1.cpu, "CPU.")
print("It is a wonderful", computer1.color, "computer.")
```

In Listing 4-10, the line *class Desktop(Computer):* denotes the beginning of an inherited class, Desktop, which inherits all of the variables of its originating class, Computer. In our example, this means strings *type* and *cpu* now become a part of class Desktop. In addition, we declare an additional variable, *color*, inside our inherited class, giving it three variables to use in total.

Naturally, inheritance in Python doesn't only apply to variables; methods are passed on as well. In Listing 4-10, *printType* is a method originating in the Computer class. However, we can summon it using an object instantiated from the Desktop class.

# Attribute Binding in Python

Let's have one more go at Python before we solemnly end the chapter (see Listing 4-11).

*Listing 4-11.* *A Python listing demonstrating ad hoc class modification*

```python
class ToiletPaper:
    pass

"Create two objects from class ToiletPaper"
type1 = ToiletPaper()
type2 = ToiletPaper()
```

```
"Add cost and brand -variables into the class"
type1.cost = 4
type1.brand = "Supersoft"
type2.cost = 2
type2.brand = "Sandpaper"

print("We sell", type1.brand, "and", type2.brand)
print("Their prices are", type1.cost, "and", type2.cost,"dollars, respectively")
```

In Listing 4-11, we use the keyword *pass* to create a class with no variables or methods. In Python, we can even instantiate these blank classes, which is what is done next. And now for the moderately fun part, say hello to ad hoc object modification. In Python, by referencing nonexistent variables within instances of blank classes, you create new data structures for said instances. We call this *attribute binding*.

Attribute binding works for classes, too (see Listing 4-12).

***Listing 4-12.*** *A Python listing demonstrating attribute binding for classes*

```
class ToiletPaper:
    pass

"Create object and add cost and brand -variables into it"
type1 = ToiletPaper()
type1.cost = 400
type1.brand ="Sandpaper"

"Add cost and brand into the class"
ToiletPaper.cost = 4
ToiletPaper.brand = "Supersoft"

"Create an object from modified class ToiletPaper"
type2 = ToiletPaper()

print("We sell", type1.brand, "for", type1.cost, "dollars")
print("We also sell", type2.brand, "for", type2.cost, "dollars")
```

Listing 4-12 starts out again by us defining an empty class. However, this time we bind attributes to this class and not only to its objects. As is evident from the listing's output, any additions of data into a class do not override an object's previous bindings.

# In Closing

Finishing this chapter, you'll have hopefully learned the following:

- The main differences between procedural and object-oriented programming (OOP) paradigms
- What abstraction, inheritance, and encapsulation refer to in the context of OOP
- How to define classes and create objects based on them in both Java and C#
- The differences between public and static methods in OOP as well as the basics of access modifiers
- What constructors are and how to use them and how to overload methods
- The basics of Unified Modeling Language (UML)

And this wraps up Chapter 4, a rather intensive part of the book. In the next chapter, we'll be wading deep into some advanced Java topics, such as file operations and multithreading.

# File Operations, Multithreading, and Other Wonders of Java

By now you're probably rather familiar with at least the basic elements of programming in the mighty object-oriented language they call Java. Now is the time to move on to more advanced concepts. We'll start off with multithreading and basic error handling in Java later in this chapter. Moving on, we'll eventually get to the jolly topic of file operations.

## Multithreading: Cores and Threads

Java supports *multithreading*, which basically refers to splitting a program in several concurrently running parts. This usually speeds up the execution time of any algorithms considerably. Multithreading is sometimes also called *concurrency*.

© Robert Ciesla 2021
R. Ciesla, *Programming Basics*, https://doi.org/10.1007/978-1-4842-7286-2_5

Multiple threads are a concept which goes hand in hand with *processor cores*, which refer to the hardware side of things: the central processor units (CPUs). An older generation, say, pre-2005 CPU typically has just one core. You're hard pressed to find a brand new single-core manufactured in 2021. Most CPUs today consist of two cores at the very minimum. These cores crunch all the data you feed into a computer (see Figure 5-1).

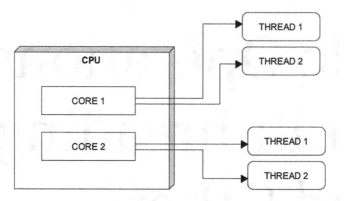

**Figure 5-1.** A simple diagram demonstrating multithreading inside a dual-core CPU

Generally speaking, the more cores your system has, the more effective its number crunching is. This depends on your operating system as well as on whether it supports multi-core computing; virtually all modern operating systems have what it takes to do so. However, not all third-party software is written to fully take advantage of multi-core processing. In that case, the software only uses a single core from the system.

Now, the number of concurrently running threads doesn't usually equal the number of cores a CPU has at its disposal. Remember, a single software application can summon numerous threads for various tasks. This means a single-core system might have several threads executing on it simultaneously. What multiple-core CPUs offer is the possibility of sharing the workload of all of these threads between numerous cores. On systems with six CPU cores or more, this can lead to tremendous boosts in computational speed.

You may come across the term *hyper-threading* every now and then. This refers to Intel's proprietary technology which, on paper, can offer double the CPU cores a processor is physically equipped with. Introduced in 2002, hyper-threading works in tandem with the operating system to increase the number of cores available. Intel claims a CPU equipped with hyper-threading offers a considerable performance boost across the board compared to an identical CPU without it. In real-life scenarios, however, the gains from hyper-threading are largely application dependent. The technology does indeed flourish under CPU-intense scenarios like video editing and 3D modeling.

# Implementing Multithreading in Java

Threads can be categorized into various states, which then constitute a *thread life cycle*. Let's next go through these five stages in detail:

1. **New**: A thread is born.

2. **Runnable**: Like the name implies, a thread in this stage is running its tasks, whichever they might be.

3. **Waiting**: A thread enters this stage when it's working with other threads and has completed their processing for the time being, letting others take the reins. A thread in this stage is awaiting the "okay" from others to resume its workload.

4. **Timed waiting**: Threads enter this stage of inaction when they have completed their task(s) for the time being, but are needed in the future at a specific point in time.

5. **Termination**: When a thread has completed all of its tasks, it dies.

---

You may have heard of *multitasking* in the context of computing. This concept refers to several processes (i.e., pieces of software) sharing the same set of resources, such as a CPU. With multithreading, tasks within a single program are split into individual threads of execution.

---

Let's glance at an actual program which demonstrates multithreading in Java (see Listing 5-1).

**Listing 5-1.** *A listing in Java demonstrating multithreading*

```
// Make HappyThreadClass inherit methods from Thread-class
// using the keyword "extends"
class HappyThreadClass extends Thread {

public HappyThreadClass(String str)
{
// The super-keyword is used to access data from a parent-class
// (Class "Thread" in this case)
super(str);
}
```

```
// Make the thread do things while executing using the run-method
public void run() {

// Iterate each thread four times, displaying each step
for (int i = 0; i < 4; i++) {
System.out.println("Step "+ i + " of " + getName());
}
System.out.println("Done processing " + getName() + "!");
}
}

public class Thread_Demo {
// Add main method
public static void main(String[] args){

// Create and execute three threads
new HappyThreadClass("Thread A").start();
new HappyThreadClass("Thread B").start();
new HappyThreadClass("Thread C").start();
}
}
```

On the second line in Listing 5-1, you'll see a new keyword, *extends*. In Java, this has a class inherit the methods and constructors of another class. In our case, *HappyThreadClass* receives the functionality of the Thread-class (referred to as *Java.lang.Thread* in the Java SDK). Later in our listing, we'll see some methods derived from thread in action, namely, the *getName( )* and *start( )* methods. The former returns a thread's name, while the latter executes a thread.

Although the output from Listing 5-1 is presented in an ordered fashion, the three threads within are run concurrently as per the approach of multithreading dictates (see Figure 5-2).

Also, upon running the listing several times in a row, you may discover the different threads display their output in differing orders. This is perfectly normal for an unsynchronized program.

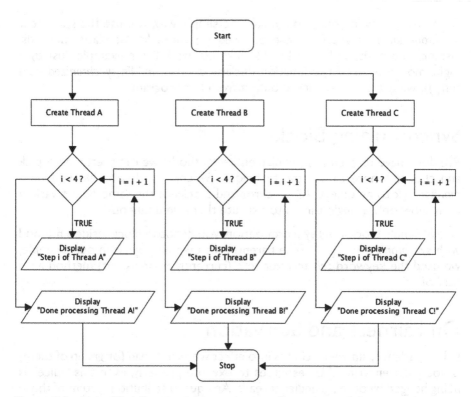

**Figure 5-2.** A simplified diagram of the programmatic flow in Listing 5-1

---

Processing power afforded by a CPU is a limited resource. Multiple threads of execution are therefore assigned *priority levels* which help your operating system prioritize their processing. This is a mostly automated process dependent on the current state of your computer's resources.

---

# Thread Synchronization

Especially in larger projects, multiple threads absolutely need to work together. Thankfully, Java takes to this approach seriously. *Thread synchronization* in the context of Java refers to controlling the access of multiple threads to a shared resource. Why synchronize at all? Well, without the approach, several threads might try to access the same data at the same time. This is not good for data ordering or stability.

To implement synchronization in Java the simple way, you use the statement *synchronized*. This approach can be used on three levels: static methods, instance methods, and code blocks. Take Listing 5-1, for example. Just by a slight modification of the function declaration (i.e., public *synchronized* void run( )), we get a more ordered output from the program.

## Synchronizing Blocks

We don't have to even synchronize entire methods; we can pretty much pick and choose where to use the technique. Synchronized code blocks bind a *monitor lock* to an object. All synchronized blocks of the same object variety then allow only a single thread to execute them simultaneously.

To add simple block-level synchronization, you denote a block inside a method with *synchronize(this)* { ... }. The parentheses take an object; in our example, we used the keyword *this* to refer to a (currently nonexistent) method it's a part of.

## On Fairness and Starvation

In Java parlance, *starvation* comes into effect when a thread (or group of them) is not given enough CPU resources to execute properly, as in this "juice" is being hogged by other, greedier threads. An equal distribution system of those precious CPU resources is called *fairness*. One of the main culprits of Java starvation lies actually in block-based synchronization. The primary way of dealing with starvation is through proper thread prioritization and the use of *locks*.

## Locks in Java

Now, every object in Java has what is known as a *lock property*. This mechanism is there to allow only those threads which are specifically granted permission to access object data. After such a thread is done working with an object, it performs a *lock release*, which returns the lock into a state of availability. Using locks is a more sophisticated form of synchronization in Java than the block-based approach (see Table 5-1).

**Table 5-1.** The main differences between block- and lock-based synchronization in Java

| | Block synchronization (e.g., *synchronize(this) ...*) | Lock-based synchronization |
|---|---|---|
| **Fairness** | Not supported | Supported |
| **Waiting state** | Cannot be interrupted | Can be interrupted |
| **Release** | Automatic | Manual |
| **Can query for lock** | No | Yes |

# Some Essential Thread Methods at a Glance

Now would be a good time to recap some key methods found in *Java.lang. Thread* (see Table 5-2). These and many other methods will become increasingly familiar to you as we proceed with this book.

**Table 5-2.** Some methods from Java's Thread-class (Java.lang.Thread)

| Method | Description | Example(s) |
|---|---|---|
| getName( ) | Returns a thread's name | System.out.println("I am a " + getName( )); |
| setPriority( ) | Sets a thread's priority. Takes a number between 1 and 10 | Orange.setPriority(10);<br>Peach.setPriority(1); |
| getPriority( ) | Returns a thread's priority | System.out.println("Priority for " + getName( ) + ": "+getPriority( )); |
| getState( ) | Returns a thread's state | State state = currentThread().getState( );<br>System.out.println("Thread: " + currentThread( ).getName( ));<br>System.out.println("State: " + state); |
| interrupt( ) | Stops a running thread | SomeClass.interrupt( ); |
| interrupted( ) | Returns whether a thread is interrupted or not | if (ShoeFactory.interrupted( ) ) {<br>System.out.println("The thread has been interrupted!"); } |
| currentThread( ) | Returns a reference to the currently executing thread | Thread gimme = Thread. currentThread( );<br>Thread niceThread = new Thread(this, "Nice Thread");<br>System.out.println("This is the " + gimme + "thread"; |

*(continued)*

**Table 5-2.** (continued)

| Method | Description | Example(s) |
|---|---|---|
| sleep( ) | Puts a thread into sleep for a specific amount of milliseconds | Thread.sleep(50); // 50 milliseconds of rest<br><br>Thread.sleep(1000); // One second nap |
| wait( ) | Puts a thread into waiting until another thread executes the notify method on it | System.out.println("Waiting..");<br><br>try {<br><br>wait();<br><br>} catch(Exception e){ } |
| notify( ) | Resumes a single thread in waiting state | synchronized(bananaObject) {<br><br>bananaObject.notify( );<br><br>System.out.println("Processing complete!"); } |
| start( ) | Executes a thread | new FruitThreads("Banana").start( );<br><br>myClass CarFactory = new myClass( );<br><br>CarFactory.start( ); |

# The Try-Catch Block

To handle errors in Java, programmers can implement the *try-catch block*. Code inside the try block is monitored for errors, and should one occur, the program switches over to code inside the catch block. This approach is also referred to as *exception handling*. Take a look at Listing 5-2 to see the mechanic in action.

**Listing 5-2.** *A simple demonstration of the try-catch block (i.e., exception handling) in Java*

```
public class TryCatchDemo {
  public static void main(String[ ] args) {
    int happyNumber = 20;

    try {
      // Divide twenty with zero (uh oh..)
      happyNumber /= 0;

      System.out.println(happyNumber);
```

```
    } catch (Exception e) {
      // Display our error message
      System.out.println("We have an error.");
    }
  }
}
```

# Finally: More Fun with Try-Catch Blocks

Yes, there's even more enjoyment to be had with Java's try-catch blocks. An optional block called *finally* is executed whether an exception comes up in the preceding try-catch or not; this is great for ensuring any specific critical actions are to be run after either event. See Listing 5-3 for a simple example of using the finally block in Java.

***Listing 5-3.*** *A Java listing demonstrating a finally block during exception handling*

```
public class TryCatchFinally
{
  public static void main (String[] args)
  {
    // Begin a try-catch block
    try {
    // happyArray is allocated to hold five integers
    // (The count starts from zero in Java)
    int happyArray[] = new int[4];

    // Be naughty and assign the value of 14 into
    // a non-existent sixth element in happyArray
    happyArray[5] = 14;
    }
    catch(ArrayIndexOutOfBoundsException e) {
    System.out.println("We encountered a medium-sized issue with an array..");
    }
    // Implement a finally-block which is executed regardless of
    // what happened in the try-catch block
    finally {
    System.out.println("You are reading this in Alan Partridge's voice!");
    }
  }
}
```

# Throw: Your Custom Error Message

To create exceptions/error messages of our own, we can use the throw statement in Java (see Listing 5-4). Using throw, we get more detailed error messages pointing out the offending lines in the code.

**Listing 5-4.** *A Java listing demonstrating the use of the throw statement*

```java
public class FruitChecker {

  // Create method for checking type of fruit
  static void checkFruit(String fruit) {

    // Display our custom error message if fruit does not equal "Lemon"
    if (!fruit.equals("Lemon")) {
      throw new RuntimeException("Only lemons are accepted.");
    }
    else {
      System.out.println("Lemon detected. Thank you!");
    }
  }

  public static void main(String[] args) {
    checkFruit("Lemon");
    checkFruit("Orange");
  }
}
```

Exceptions in Java are basically signals that something has gone wrong during the execution of a program. There are numerous types of exceptions available for the programmer to implement.

In Listing 5-4, the term *RuntimeException* refers to a general type of error; we chose to throw one out in case we don't encounter a lemon. Since we run the checkFruit() method for both a "Lemon" and an "Orange," we get both an exception-free message as well as one with an exception. See the output from Listing 5-4:

Lemon detected. Thank you!

Exception in thread "main" java.lang.RuntimeException: Only lemons are accepted.

```
    at FruitChecker.checkFruit(FruitChecker.java:8)
    at FruitChecker.main(FruitChecker.java:17)
```

Let's take a look at some other common exceptions available in Java next:

- **ArrayIndexOutOfBoundsException**: This exception is thrown when accessing an item of an array at an index which is not there (i.e., the index is outside of the allocated size of an array).

- **ArithmeticException**: Thrown when an arithmetic operation fails.

- **ClassNotFoundException**: As you might guess, this is thrown when trying to access a class that is nowhere to be found.

- **NumberFormatException**: Thrown when a method is unable to convert a string into a numeral.

- **NoSuchFieldException**: Thrown when addressing a variable that is missing from a class.

- **RuntimeException**: As seen in Listing 5-3, this exception is be used for any general error during program execution.

# Checked and Unchecked Exceptions

There are basically two categories of exceptions in Java: *checked* and *unchecked*. The former is used when addressing errors found outside of the program's grasp, for example, issues with file operations or network transfers. Unchecked exceptions, sometimes also called *runtime exceptions*, deal with problems within the programming logic such as invalid arguments and unsupported operations. See Table 5-3 for a more detailed rundown on the differences between these two types of exceptions.

**Table 5-3.** The main differences between checked and unchecked exceptions in Java

|  | Checked exceptions | Unchecked/runtime exceptions |
|---|---|---|
| **Main area of effect** | External, outside of program | Internal, within program |
| **Examples** | Issues with file access or network connectivity, problems with external databases | Flawed programmatic logic; errors with class definitions, arithmetic operations, or variable conversions |
| **Detection** | During compilation of program | During program execution |
| **Priority level** | Critical: cannot be ignored. Program will fail to execute | Severe: should not be ignored |
|  |  | Program will run, but remains more or less unstable |

We'll go into even more detail with Java's quite exceptional exception handling later in the book.

# Basic File Operations in Java

Basically, file operations refer to the reading, writing, and deletion of data stored on a device such as a hard disk or a solid state drive. To set up a Java project ready for file operations, we should add the following package into the beginning of a listing: *import java.io.File*. In fact, let's see what a simple file operation program in Java looks like (see Listing 5-5).

**Listing 5-5.** *A Java listing for creating an empty text file*

```java
import java.io.File;
public class JollyFileClass {

  public static void main(String[] args) {
    // Use the imported File class to create a file object, happyfile
    File happyfile = new File("apress_is_great.txt");

    // Begin a try-catch block
    try {
      // Summon the createNewFile-method from File class
      boolean ok = happyfile.createNewFile();
      // ok is a boolean variable, meaning it holds either 'true' or 'false'
      if (ok == true) {
        System.out.println("File " + happyfile.getName() + " created.");
      }
      else {
        System.out.println("The file already exists.");
      }
    }
    // Display error message in the catch-block if necessary
    catch(Exception e) {
    System.out.println("We have an issue..");
    }
  }
}
```

Not just limited to the methods we examined in Listing 5-5, the java.io.File-package offers much more. See Table 5-4 for all of the methods we'll be exploring soon. Also, Table 5-5 lists some of the time-related formatting markers we'll be delving into later in the chapter. Java's formatting markers display time and dates parsed into specific string patterns. For now, it suffices you're aware of them; many of them originate in the class *java.time.format.DateTimeFormatter*.

**Table 5-4.** *Some common methods for file operations in Java provided by java.io.File*

| createNewFile( ) | Creates a new file | length( ) | Returns a file's size in bytes |
|---|---|---|---|
| mkdir( ) | Makes a new directory | getAbsolutePath( ) | Retrieves the absolute path of a file, e.g., C:\Windows\hello.txt |
| delete( ) | Deletes a file | canRead( ) | Tests if a file is readable or not |
| exists( ) | Tests if a file exists | canWrite( ) | Tests if a file is writeable or not |

# Creating Text Files in Java

Getting right back to it, let's make a text file next, shall we? See Listing 5-6 for our next dose of Java file operation goodness.

**Listing 5-6.** *A Java program demonstrating text-file creation and access*

```java
import java.io.*;

public class Main {
  public static void main(String args[]) {

    // Define a string we intend to write into a file
    String data = "Apress rules, OK?";

    try {
      // Create a Writer object using the FileWriter-class
      FileWriter writer1 = new FileWriter("happyfile.txt");
      // Writes a message to the file
      writer1.write(data);
      // Closes the writer
      writer1.close();
      // Open the created file
      File file1 = new File("happyfile.txt");
      // Create a new file input stream, "fileinput1"
      FileInputStream fileinput1 = new FileInputStream(file1);
System.out.println("The file " + file1.getName() + " says the following:");

int counter=0;
// Use a while-loop to display every text character in "happyfile.txt"
// Break out of "while" when encountering "-1", which signals the
// end of the file
while((counter = fileinput1.read())!=-1)
{
System.out.print((char)counter);
}
```

```
        // Close file input stream
        fileinput1.close();
        }
        catch (Exception e) {
          e.getStackTrace();
        }
    }
}
```

In the second listing, you'll see a plethora of new, and potentially frightening, mechanics. We'll now go through them in a calm manner, one by one. First off, *import java.io.\*;* is in Listing 5-6 to provide access to all of the classes available in the java.io-package.

Next, we have the Filewriter class. As you might predict, this class provides the means to write data and create new files. We instantiate an object from Filewriter, giving it the name *happyfile.txt.*

---

In Listing 5-6, we provide both a filename and a *directory path* for our file to be, *happyfile.txt.* The part with the letter C refers to the most common choice of the Windows root drive. You are good running this listing in an online programming environment. However, you are not likely to actually write anything to your hard drive if you use one.

---

Moving down the listing, we summon the write method from the Filewriter class, passing to it the message from the string *data.* Our happyfile.txt now has a text-based message in it. Next up, we execute the close method; this needs to be done in order for subsequent methods to gain access to happyfile.txt.

Now, we open our file again, this time for printing its contents on screen. We do this by first instantiating an object using Java's File class, that is, *File file1 = new File("c:\\happyfile.txt").* The line *FileInputStream fileinput1 = new FileInputStream(file1)* gives us access to the Java file input stream class, providing file reading capabilities in one-byte increments. In our case, this means reading and displaying a text file (i.e., happyfile.txt) one character at a time. For this, we implement a while loop which uses a method (i.e., *read*) from the FileInputStream class.

We print the contents of happyfile.txt (again, one character at a time, as per how FileInputStream file access is implemented). A value of negative one (-1) signals the end of the file, breaking us out of the while loop. After this, it's just cleanup time. We close the file and exit the program.

# More Adventures in Java File Operations

Let's do some more file manipulation. How about we query file attributes, such as file size, and experiment in some file deletion as well (see Listing 5-7).

*Listing 5-7. A program demonstrating file attribute query and deletion in Java*

```java
import java.io.*;

public class Main2 {
  public static void main(String args[]) {
    // Open file for access
    File file1 = new File("c:\\happyfile.txt");
    // Begin try-catch block
    try {
      // First check if file exists
      if (file1.exists()) {
      // If so, display confirmation of existence
      System.out.println("The file " + file1.getName() + " exists!");
      // Summon length()-method and display file size
      System.out.println("This file is " + file1.length() + " bytes in size");
      // Display notification if the file is over 10 bytes/characters in size
      if(file1.length()>10) System.out.println("That's a lot of data!");
      // Display read/write information
      if (file1.canRead()) System.out.println("This file is readable.");
      if (file1.canWrite()) System.out.println("This file is writable.");
      System.out.println("Deleting " + file1.getName() + "...");
      // Summon delete()-method on file1
      file1.delete();
          // If file does not exist, display notification
      } else System.out.println("Can't find file. Nothing will be deleted.");
      }
      catch (Exception e) {
        e.getStackTrace();
      }
  }
}
```

As you can see from Listing 5-7, implementing basic file operations in Java is rather straightforward. But there's a few operations we should still experiment with. How about we use a second type of file stream—and create a brand new directory, too? (See Listing 5-8.)

**Listing 5-8.** *A listing in Java demonstrating the use of file streams and directories*

```java
import java.io.*;
class FileStreamTesting {
   public static void main(String args[]) {
      // Begin try-catch block
      try {
      // Define a string we use as a name for a directory
      String directoryName = "HappyDirectory";
      File dir1 = new File(directoryName);
      // Create new directory into the Windows root-folder, C:
      dir1.mkdir();
      // Create an array of six characters, Publisher
      char Publisher[] = {'A','p','r','e','s','s'};
      // Instantiate an object from the OutputStream class, stream1
OutputStream stream1= new FileOutputStream("c://HappyDirectory//
publisher.txt");
         for(int x = 0; x < Publisher.length ; x++) {
            // Write each character from our array into the file
            stream1.write(Publisher[x]);
         }
         stream1.close();

      } catch (IOException e) {
         System.out.print("An error has occurred.");
      }
   }
}
```

The last two listings made use of Java's file streaming classes. Listing 5-7 used a method from the InputStream class to print text on screen. In Listing 5-8, we have an instance of Java's OutputStream writing an array of six characters (i.e., the contents of *Publisher[ ]*) into a file.

When specifying a directory location, the two listings had differing notation: in Listing 5-7, we used a backslash (i.e., *c:\\happyfile.txt*) to denote a directory path, while in Listing 5-8, we went with the forward slash, as in *c://HappyDirectory*. Both approaches should work in Java.

# Java Dating

Let's face it: keeping track of time in this world is rather important. There's no reason to not do it in Java as well. Luckily, there's a great class for that, known as *LocalDate*. Also, the *java.time.format.DateTimeFormatter* class is there to display dates as per a custom formatting pattern defined by you, the programmer. (we encountered these formatting markers in Table 5-5). Listing 5-9 is here to show you how this is done.

**Listing 5-9.** *A program demonstrating date retrieval and formatting in Java*

```java
import java.time.LocalDate;
import java.time.format.DateTimeFormatter;
public class HappyDateDemo {
    public static void main(String args[]) {
        // Create an object using the Java LocalDate-class
        LocalDate happyDate = LocalDate.now();
        LocalDate fortnite = happyDate.minusDays(14);
        LocalDate tomorrow = happyDate.plusDays(14);
        System.out.println("Today's date is " + happyDate);
        System.out.println("Two weeks ago it was " + fortnite);
        System.out.println("Two weeks into the future it'll be.. " + tomorrow);
        // Create and display three different formatting patterns
        System.out.println("Today's date in format A: "+happyDate.
        format(DateTimeFormatter.ofPattern("d.M.uuuu")));
        System.out.println("Today's date in format B: "+happyDate.
        format(DateTimeFormatter.ofPattern("MMM d uuuu")));
        System.out.println("Today's date in format C: "+happyDate.
        format(DateTimeFormatter.ofPattern("d.MMM.uu")));
    }
}
```

**Table 5-5.** Some time pattern–formatting markers from java.time.format.
DateTimeFormatter

| | | | |
|---|---|---|---|
| *d/dd* | Day of the month | *W* | Week in a month (0–5) |
| *MM* | Month | *K* | Hour in a day (1–24) |
| *uuuu/uu* | Year (full or last two digits) | *K* | Hour in a day, AM/PM (0–11) |
| *w* | Week in a year (1–53) | *E* | Day of the week (e.g., Monday) |

# More on Dating: Leap Years and Time Travel

Let's explore more of Java's dating options. Not only can we travel back and forward in time using a day as a unit; months and years are also at our disposal. See Listing 5-10 for an example of these two in action. Also, we'll be exploring how to discover leap years in Java.

**Listing 5-10.** *A listing demonstrating the use of some of the methods in the LocalDate class in Java*

```java
import java.time.LocalDate;
import java.time.LocalTime;

public class TimeTravel {
public static void main(String[] args) {
// Store current date into rightnow
LocalDate rightnow = LocalDate.now();
System.out.println("This is thirty weeks into the future: " + rightnow.
plusWeeks(30));
System.out.println("This is fifty months into the past: " + rightnow.
minusMonths(50));
System.out.println("This is 56 years into the past: " + rightnow.
minusYears(56));
System.out.println("Whoa! This is 373 years into the future: " + rightnow.
plusYears(373));
// Store a future date into futuredate1
LocalDate futuredate1 = LocalDate.of(2028,1,1);
// Store a past date into pastdate1
LocalDate pastdate1 = LocalDate.of(1728,1,1);
// Check for leap years
System.out.println("\nWas the year " + pastdate1.getYear() + " a leap year? "
+ pastdate1.isLeapYear());
System.out.println("Is the year " + rightnow.getYear() + " a leap year? " +
rightnow.isLeapYear());
System.out.println("Is the year " + futuredate1.getYear() + " a leap year? "
+ futuredate1.isLeapYear());
    }
}
```

# Calendars in Java

There are many approaches when it comes to time travel in Java, specifically within the Gregorian calendar which remains the most popular system of organizing our days since 1582. We may fetch past and future date rather easily, as demonstrated by Listing 5-11.

**Listing 5-11.** *A listing demonstrating the use of the Calendar class in Java*

```java
import java.util.Calendar;
public class HappyCalendar {

    public static void main(String[] args) {
    // Create an object using the Calendar-class
    Calendar calendar1 = Calendar.getInstance();
    // Display current date
```

```
System.out.println("Current date: " + calendar1.getTime());
// Take a week out of the date and display it
calendar1.add(Calendar.DATE, -7);
System.out.println("A week ago it was: " + calendar1.getTime());
// Fast forward two months
calendar1.add(Calendar.MONTH, 2);
System.out.println("Two months into the future: " + calendar1.getTime());
// Go ten years into the future
calendar1.add(Calendar.YEAR, 10);
System.out.println("Ten years into the future: " + calendar1.getTime());
// Go a century back into the past
calendar1.add(Calendar.YEAR, -100);
System.out.println("A century ago: " + calendar1.getTime());
  }
}
```

# Customizing Your Calendar

Fun with Java-based calendars doesn't stop at time travel. Let's make things truly interesting and create our own date format symbols, that is, weekdays and months. For this, we're summoning some exciting new methods and a new class, *Locale* (see Listing 5-12). You'll notice this listing imports the class java.util.Date. This is a so-called deprecated class, meaning a more up-to-date version of it exists (in this case java.util.LocalDate). However, you may come across these more historical classes in your coding adventures from time to time.

**Listing 5-12.** *A Java listing demonstrating customized date symbol creation for a particular locale*

```
import java.text.DateFormatSymbols;
import java.util.Date;
import java.util.Locale;
import java.text.SimpleDateFormat;

public class SassyCalendar {

public static void main(String [] args){
// Create a new object from class Locale
Locale locale1 = new Locale("en", "US");
// Create an object for a new set of date format symbols
DateFormatSymbols sassysymbols = new DateFormatSymbols(locale1);
```

```
// Rename days of the week using setWeekdays() method
sassysymbols.setWeekdays(new String[]{
        "",
        "Superior Sunday",
        "Mega Monday",
        "Tepid Tuesday",
        "Wonderful Wednesday",
        "Tedious Thursday",
        "Fun Friday",
        "Serious Saturday",
});
// Rename months using setMonths() method
sassysymbols.setMonths(new String[]{
        "",
        "Jolly January", "Fabulous February",
        "Marvelous March", "Amazing April",
        "Joyous June", "Jubilant July",
        "Affable August", "Silly September",
        "Odorous October", "Nasty November",
        "Delightful December",
});
// Choose a formatting pattern
String pattern = "EEEEE', in 'MMMMM yyyy'!'";
// Apply this pattern on our object, sassysymbols
SimpleDateFormat format1 = new SimpleDateFormat(pattern, sassysymbols);
// Create a new object using Date-class
String sassydate = format1.format(new Date());
System.out.println("Today is " + sassydate);
    }
}
```

In Listing 5-12, we catered to a specific locale, the United States, choosing English as the language using the expressions "US" and "en." We'll get more into localization later in this chapter.

Now, the methods *setWeekdays( )* and *setMonths( )* both accept arrays of strings, which are used to override the default formatting symbols (e.g., Monday, January, etc.). The first item in these arrays is left intentionally blank as it doesn't factor into the workings of these methods.

When it comes to the formatting pattern in Listing 5-12, we use *E* to denote the (now modified) day of the week, *M* for month, and *y* for year. We also added a bit of space and other punctuation inside single quotation marks (e.g., ' ! ').

If we run Listing 5-12 on the, say, 29th of June 2021, we would get the following output:

Today is Tepid Tuesday, in Joyous June 2021!

# Internationalization and Localization in Java

*Internationalization* refers to designing software so that it can be localized without major overhaul; *localization* is the act of creating content for a specific language and/or region. Java is a great programming language when it comes to internationalization, offering the means to localize dates, currencies, and numbers rather dynamically.

---

The term "internationalization" can be a tad cumbersome to type. Hence, software folks sometimes prefer the abbreviation *i18n* instead. Localization, on the other hand, is referred to as *L10n* among people in the know. Like you may have guessed, the numbers in these abridgements represent the amount of letters in the aforementioned two terms.

---

The Java Locale class, as briefly touched upon in Listing 5-12, offers options when it comes to localizing our projects. It's there to give programmers the opportunity to present localized messages or other parts of a program. The Locale class is used to identify objects while not being a container for objects themselves.

The Locale class works with three dimensions: *language*, *country*, and *variant*. While the first two are self-explanatory, variant is used for things like the type and/or version of an operating system the program runs on.

Now, in Java, an application can actually have several locales active at the same time. For example, it's possible to combine an Italian date format and a Japanese number format. Therefore, Java is a good choice for creating truly multicultural applications. Let's peek at Listing 5-13 for a demonstration on how to use localization in Java.

***Listing 5-13.*** *A listing demonstrating the three main dimensions of locales in Java (i.e., language, country, and variant)*

```java
import java.util.Locale;

public class LocalizationDemo {
 public static void main(String[] args) {

    // Create a generic English-speaking locale
    Locale locale1 = new Locale("en");
    // Create an English-speaking locale set in the UK
    Locale locale2 = new Locale("en", "UK");
    // Create a Finnish-speaking, Indian locale in Mumbai
    Locale locale3 = new Locale("fi", "IN", "Mumbai");
```

```
System.out.println("Locale 1. " + locale1.getDisplayName());
System.out.println("Locale 2. " + locale2.getDisplayName());
System.out.println("Locale 3. " + locale3.getDisplayName());

// Retrieve user's current operating system locale information by creating
// another instance of Locale-class and summoning the getDefault() method
Locale yourLocale = Locale.getDefault();

System.out.println("OS language: " + yourLocale.getDisplayLanguage());
System.out.println("OS country: " + yourLocale.getDisplayCountry());
 }
}
```

In Listing 5-13, we start off by creating three different objects of locale and display some of their contents using the *getDisplayName( )* method found in the Locale class.

We also summon a fourth object for examining the user's operating system's locale settings. First, the *getDefault( )* method is used to retrieve this data and insert it into the object we named *yourLocale*. Then, two other methods are executed, namely, *getDisplayLanguage( )* and *getDisplayCountry( )*, to display the information we're interested in.

# In Closing

Finishing this chapter, you'll have hopefully learned the following:

- How to open, create, and delete files with Java
- What multithreading refers to and how it's implemented in Java
- How to implement basic synchronization in Java
- The operation of the try-catch block
- What exception handling means and how it's implemented
- The difference between checked and unchecked exceptions
- Some basic use of date-related classes in Java
- The basics of Java-based localization

Chapter 6 will offer something indeed completely different; we'll be exploring the more advanced functionalities of the puissant Python language.

# And Now for Something Completely Different: Advanced Python

After immersing ourselves deeper in the world of Java in the previous chapter, it's time to do the same with Python. We'll start off with file operations, moving on to multithreading and other more advanced topics

© Robert Ciesla 2021
R. Ciesla, *Programming Basics*, https://doi.org/10.1007/978-1-4842-7286-2_6

later in this chapter. The purpose here is to give you a solid foundation on some of the deeper mechanics in Python for you to build on later according to your needs.

# Python File Operations

To open files in Python, we use the sensibly named *open( )* function. It uses the following syntax: *file-object name = open(filename, access_mode, buffering)*. The last two attributes are optional. A simple example of Python's open( ) function could look like this:

```
happyfile = open("happytext.txt")
```

Now, Python uses what are known as *access modes* for its file operations. Not all files need to be written or appended to when sometimes all you need to do is to read from one. See Table 6-1 for a list of Python's file access modes.

**Table 6-1.** The twelve Python file-access modes

| | | | |
|---|---|---|---|
| r | Opens a file in read-only mode. This is the default access mode in Python | w+ | Opens a file in read/write mode; overwrites file if it already exists |
| rb | Opens a file in read-only binary mode | wb+ | Opens a file in read/write binary mode; overwrites file if it already exists |
| r+ | Opens a file in read/write mode | a | Opens a file for appending into. If file does not exist, one is created |
| rb+ | Opens a file in read/write binary mode | ab | Opens a binary file for appending into. If file does not exist, one is created |
| w | Opens a file in write-only mode; overwrites file if it already exists | a+ | Opens a file for both appending and reading. If file does not exist, one is created |
| wb | Opens a file in write-only binary mode; overwrites file if it already exists | ab+ | Opens a file for both appending and reading in binary mode. If file does not exist, one is created |

*Buffering* in the context of Python's file operations refers to the process of storing a part of a file in a temporary memory area until the file is completely loaded. Basically, a value of zero (0) switches buffering off, while one (1) enables it, for example, *somefile = open("nobuffer.txt", "r", 1)*. If no value is given, Python uses your system's default setting. Usually it's a good idea to keep buffering on for a speed boost in file operations.

# File Attributes in Python

There are basically four main file attributes in Python (one of which is mostly of historical interest, i.e., *softspace*). You're likely to get well acquainted with all of them if your projects include even the smallest amount of file operations. See Table 6-2 for a rundown of these attributes in Python.

**Table 6-2.** The four Python file-object attributes

| Attribute | Description | Example |
|---|---|---|
| .name | Returns a file name | happyfile = open("happytext.txt")<br>print(happyfile.name) |
| .mode | Returns file access mode | anotherfile = open("whackytext.txt")<br>print(anotherfile.mode) |
| .closed | Returns "true" if file closed | apress_file = open("supertext.txt")<br>apress_file.close( )<br>    if print(apress_file.closed):<br>    print("File closed!") |
| .softspace | Returns "false" if print statements are to have a space character inserted before first item. Historical: obsolete since Python 3.0 | file5 = open("jollyfile.txt")<br>print("Softspace set? ",<br>file5.softspace) |

# Practical File Access

A file needs to remain open in Python for it to be manipulated; a file set to closed cannot be written to or have its attributes examined. See Listing 6-1 for a demonstration on file access and how to read file attributes in Python.

***Listing 6-1.*** *A listing in Python demonstrating some basic file operations*

```
# Import a special module, time, for the sleep() method
import time
file1 = open("apress.txt", "wb") # Create/open file
print("File-name: ", file1.name) # Start reading file attributes
print("Opening mode: ", file1.mode)
print("Is file closed? ", file1.closed)
time.sleep(1) # Sleep/delay for one second, for the suspense
file1.close() # Close file
print("Now we closed the file..");
time.sleep(1.5) # Sleep/delay for 1.5 seconds
print("File is closed now? ", file1.closed)
```

# Directory Operations in Python

A directory or folder is an important part of any operating system's file management system; Python, too, offers ways of working with them. Let's take a gander at some directory operations next (see Listing 6-2).

*Listing 6-2.* *A listing in Python demonstrating directory operations*

```
import os # import the os module for directory operations
print("Current directory:", os.getcwd()) # Print current directory using getcwd()
print("List of files:", os.listdir()) # List files in directory using listdir()
os.chdir('C:\\') # Change to the (most common) Windows root-directory
print("New directory location:", os.getcwd()) # Print current directory again

print("Let's make a new directory and call it JollyDirectory")
os.mkdir('JollyDirectory') # Make a new directory using mkdir()
print("List of files in JollyDirectory:", os.listdir('JollyDirectory'))
```

As for renaming a directory, we would use *os.rename("Somedirectory", "Newname")*. Once a directory is no longer needed, and is empty of files first, it only takes *os.rmdir("Somedirectory")* to remove it.

# File Name Pattern Matching

We have ways of locating files matching specific naming patterns in Python. These are rather simple to implement as is evident from Listing 6-3.

*Listing 6-3.* *A listing in Python demonstrating file name pattern matching*

```
import os
import fnmatch

# Display all files in Windows root with .txt/.rtf extension
for filename in os.listdir('C:\\'):
    if filename.endswith('.txt') or filename.endswith('.rtf'):
        print(filename)
# Display all files with .txt extension starting with 'a'
for filename in os.listdir('C:\\'):
    if fnmatch.fnmatch(filename, 'a*.txt'):
        print(filename)
```

In Listing 6-3, we introduced two handy functions for locating files with specific naming conventions, namely, *endswith()* and *fnmatch()*. The latter provides so-called wildcard-based searches into your Python projects (e.g., *file\*.txt* or *????name.txt*).

# File Searching with Glob?

The term *globbing* refers to performing highly exactfile searches inside specific directories (or Python's current working directory if none are specified). The term *glob*, short for *global*, has its origins in the world of Unix-based operating systems. In Listing 6-4, you'll see this approach put to good use.

**Listing 6-4.** *A listing in Python demonstrating file searches by globbing*

```python
import glob
# Using * pattern
print("\nGlobbing with wildcard pattern * (*.py)")
for name in glob.glob("*.py"):
    print(name)
# Using ? pattern
print("\nGlobbing with wildcard ? and * (??????.*)")
for name in glob.glob("??????.*"):
    print(name)
# Using [0-9] pattern
print("\nGlobbing with wildcard range [0-9]")
for name in glob.glob("*[0-9].*"):
    print(name)
# Using [b-x] pattern
print("\nGlobbing with wildcard range [b-x]")
for name in glob.glob("*[b-x].*"):
    print(name)
```

# Dates in Python

You may remember the rather robust facilities for displaying time and calendar data in Java in the previous chapter. Python offers just as much when it comes to time keeping. These functionalities reside in the datetime module (see Listing 6-5).

**Listing 6-5.** *A listing demonstrating some time and calendar functions in Python*

```python
import datetime
from datetime import timedelta

time1 = datetime.datetime.now() # Create a datetime-object for right now
print("The time is:", time1) # Display current time unformatted
# Display formatted day and month (%A for day of the week, %B for month)
print("In other words it's a", time1.strftime("%A in %B"))
# Reduce time1.year-variable by ten
print("Ten years ago it was", time1.year-10)
```

```
# Use timedelta to move thirty days into the future
futuredate = datetime.timedelta(days=30)
futuredate += time1 # Add the current date to futuredate
print("Thirty days into the future it'll be", futuredate.strftime("%B"))
```

While Listing 6-5 is rather straightforward, we should take a better look at some formatting markers available in Python for all your date-related needs (see Table 6-3).

**Table 6-3.** Some common date-formatting markers in Python

| | | | |
|---|---|---|---|
| %A | Full day of the week (e.g., Monday) | %B | Full name of month (e.g., March) |
| %a | Short day of the week (e.g., Mon) | %b | Short name of month (e.g., Mar) |
| %Z | Time zone (e.g., UTC) | %H | Hour, 24h system (e.g., 18) |
| %p | AM/PM | %I | Hour, 12h system |

# The Majesty of Regular Expressions

A *regular expression*, often shortened to *RegEx*, is a sequence of characters that constitutes a search pattern for strings. Importing a code module simply called *re* allows us to perform RegEx work in Python. You can use regular expressions to locate files with a very specific search pattern, as well as seek specific terms inside numerous types of text files. See Listing 6-6 for a first demonstration on how they work.

**Listing 6-6.** *A simple example of using regular expressions in Python*

```
import re
text1 = "Apress is the best publisher"
regex1 = re.findall("es", text1) # Create a RegEx-object with search-pattern
print("Looking for all instances of 'es'")
print("We found", len(regex1), "matches in", text1)
```

In Listing 6-6, we summoned the findall method to look for instances of "es" in string-variable *text1*. We also used Python's len() method to count the instances stored in list *regex1*. Now, it's time to peek at another demonstration of RegEx magic (see Listing 6-7).

---

Regular expressions actually date back to 1951, when they were introduced by American mathematician *Stephen Cole Kleene (1909–1994)*. Nowadays, regular expressions are a staple in many popular programming languages, including Perl, C#, and Java. RegEx implementation in the latter two languages will be explored later in this book.

---

***Listing 6-7.*** *A listing in Python demonstrating search( ) and fullmatch( ) RegEx methods in Python*

```python
import re
# Summon search-method from the regex module, re
match1 = re.search('Apress', 'Apress is the best')
if match1: # This is shorthand for "if match1 == True:"
    print(match1) # Display object contents if match found

happytext = "My name is Jimmy" # Create a string variable
match2 = re.search('Jimmy', happytext)
if match2:
    print(match2)

# Use fullmatch-method from re on string "happytext"
match3 = re.fullmatch('Jimmy', happytext)
if match3:
    print("Match found for 'Jimmy'!") # This message will not display
else:
    print("No Match for 'Jimmy'")

match3 = re.fullmatch('My name is Jimmy', happytext)
if match3:
    print(match3)

# Use match-method
match4 = re.match('the', 'Apress is the best')
if match4:
    print(match4) # This message will not display
    # match() only looks for patterns from the beginning of a string
else:
    print("No Match for 'the'")
match5 = re.match('Apress', 'Apress is the best')
if match5:
    print(match5) # This message will display
```

In Listing 6-7, we used search( ), match( ), and fullmatch( ). You might ask what the differences between them are. The search method goes through an entire string for a given pattern, while fullmatch only returns true if a string completely mirrors a pattern. The match method looks for patterns at the beginning of a string only.

# Metacharacters

Regular expressions are best used with *metacharacters*. These are basically the building blocks for more advanced string-related searches. See Table 6-4 for a rundown of some important metacharacters and Listing 6-8 for a little demonstration of their use.

**Table 6-4.** Some important Python metacharacters

| \w | Any word. Usually refers to alphanumericals | \s | Whitespace |
|---|---|---|---|
| \W | Any non-word | \S | Non-whitespace |
| \d | Any digit | . | Any single character |
| \D | Any non-digit | * | Zero or more characters |

*Listing 6-8.* *A listing in Python demonstrating the use of metacharacters in regular expressions*

```python
import re
match1 = re.search('.....', 'Hello there!')
if match1: # This is shorthand for "if match1 == True:"
    print(match1) # Displays "Hello"

match2 = re.search('\d..', 'ABC123')
if match2:
    print(match2) # Displays "123"

match3 = re.search('\D*', 'My name is Reginald123456.')
if match3:
    print(match3) # Displays "My name is Reginald"

match4 = re.search('y *\w*', 'Hello. How are you?')
if match4:
    print(match4) # Displays "you"

match5 = re.search('\S+', 'Hello. Whats up?')
if match5:
    print(match5) # Displays "Hello."
```

In Listing 6-8, with *match4*, we're using the metacharacter \w which refers to seeking matches with any full words. Without this character in place, we'd see an output of "y" instead of "you."

Let's learn some more about metacharacters in Python. See Table 6-5 for eight more important RegEx markers and Listing 6-9 for a second demonstration.

**Table 6-5.** Some more important Python metacharacters

| \. | Literal dot (as in, a full stop character) | $ | Match end of line |
|---|---|---|---|
| ? | Zero or one character | { n } | Occurs for n times |
| + | One or more characters | [a-z] | Character set |
| ^ | Match beginning of line | [0-9] | Numeric character set |

**Listing 6-9.** *Another listing in Python demonstrating the use of metacharacters in regular expressions*

```python
import re
string1 = 'Beezow Doo-doo Zopittybop-bop-bop'
patterns = [r'Do*', # D and zero or more o's (*)
            r'Be+', # B and one or more e's (+)
            r'Do?', # D and zero or one o's (?)
            r'it{2}', # i and two t's
            r'[BDZ]\w*', # Look for full words starting with B, D, or Z
            r'^Be\w*', # Look for a full word starting with "Be"
            r'...$' # Look for the three last digits in the string
            ]
def discover_patterns(patterns, string1): # Create our method
    for pattern in patterns:
        newpattern = re.compile(pattern) # Summon compile()
        print('Looking for {} in'.format(pattern), string1)
        print(re.findall(newpattern, string1)) # Summon findall()
discover_patterns(patterns, string1) # Execute our method
```

The list-structure *patterns* in Listing 6-9 contain seven searches, while *string1* stores our source material. These two data structures are to be fed into the method *discover_patterns* which we created next.

Inside this new method of ours, we use two of Python's RegEx functions: *compile( )* and *findall( )*. With the former, we are converting RegEx patterns into pattern objects, which are then used for pattern matching. This approach is most efficient in scenarios where search patterns are to be reused, such as database access.

Findall is used to discover all occurrences of a search pattern inside strings. The *r'* in our listing lets Python know a string is considered a "raw string," meaning backlashes in it will be interpreted without special functions. For example, \n will not denote a newline in a raw string.

# More Merriment with Regular Expressions

Let's explore yet more of the advanced features of RegEx next. Listing 6-10 exhibits the use of two new methods: *group( )* and *sub( )* (displayed in bold for your convenience). In addition, we'll be using a new technique with our old friend in RegEx, search( ).

**Listing 6-10.** *A listing in Python demonstrating the sub( ) method*

```
import re
string1 = "Today's dessert: banana"
# Summon search() with four options for a match
choice1 = re.search(r"dessert.*(noni-fruit|banana|cake|toilet-paper)", string1)
if choice1:
    print("You'll be having this for", choice1.group(), "!")

string2 = "Have a great day"
string2 = re.sub('great', 'wonderful', string2)
print(string2) # Outputs: Have a wonderful day

string3 = 'what is going on?'
# Replace all letters between a and h with a capital X
string3 = re.sub('([a-h])s*', 'X', string3)
print(string3) # Outputs: wXXt is XoinX on?
```

The search method in Listing 6-10 is used to compare and locate strings that are listed now as the method's arguments. In other words, *string1* is searched for a total of four varieties of fruit. These are separated by the logical or operator, denoted by the vertical line character (i.e., |). The method is made to look out for any of these strings/fruit, but only should they appear next to the string "dessert." If there's such a match between string1 and an item in choice1, the program displays it.

# Concurrency and Parallelism in Python

*Parallel processing* refers to executing more than one calculation or instruction at the same time. You may remember the concept of multithreading from the previous chapter. Like Java and C#, Python is capable of processing multiple threads of execution. However, there are some major differences. Python's multithreading does not actually run threads in a parallel fashion. Rather, it executes these threads pseudo-concurrently. This stems from Python's implementation of a *global interpreter lock (GIL)*. This mechanism is there to synchronize threads and make sure the entire Python project is executed only on a single CPU; it simply does not utilize the full oomph of multi-core processors.

---

Although *concurrency* and *parallelism* are related terms, they are not one and the same. The former refers to the approach of running separate tasks simultaneously, while with the latter, a task is split into subtasks which are then executed at the same time.

---

# Multiprocessing vs. Multithreading

Actual parallel processing of threads in Python is achieved through the use of multiple processes, all with their own interpreter and GIL. This is known as *multiprocessing*.

Python's take on concurrency can be a somewhat complicated one (compared to, say, Java). Now, a *process* in Python is not the same as a *thread*. Although both are independent sequences of code execution, there are several differences. A process tends to use more system memory than a thread. A process's life cycle is generally also slower to manage; its creation and deletion take more resources. See Table 6-6 for a comparison of threads and processes.

**Table 6-6.** The main differences between threads and processes in Python (i.e., multiprocessing vs. multithreading)

|  | **Process** | **Thread** |
|---|---|---|
| Uses single global interpreter lock (GIL) | No | Yes |
| Multiple CPU cores and/or CPUs | Supported | Not supported |
| Code complexity | Less complicated | More complicated |
| RAM footprint | Heavier | Lighter |
| Can be interrupted/ killed | Yes | No |
| Works best for | CPU-heavy applications, 3D rendering, scientific modeling, data mining, cryptocurrencies | User interfaces, network applications |

Python has three code modules for simultaneous processing: multiprocessing, asyncio, and threading. For CPU-intensive tasks, the multiprocessing module works best.

# Implementing Multithreading in Python

Multithreading in Python goes hand in hand with the global interpreter lock (GIL) mechanism as discussed earlier in this chapter. This approach uses the principle of *mutual exclusion* (see Figure 6-1). Since the scheduling in Python's multithreading is done by the operating system, some overhead (i.e., delay) is inevitable; this is something multiprocessing generally doesn't suffer from.

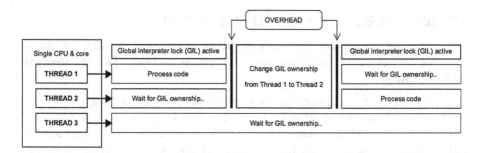

**Figure 6-1.** A partial visualization of multithreading in Python using three threads

It's time to get practical. Let's examine how multithreading is implemented in Python (see Listing 6-11).

**Listing 6-11.** A listing in Python demonstrating elementary use of the threading module

```python
import threading
def happy_multiply(num, num2):
    print("Multiply", num, "with", num2, "=", (num * num2))
def happy_divide(num, num2):
    print("Divide", num, "with", num2, "=", (num / num2))

if __name__ == "__main__":
    # Create two threads
    thread1 = threading.Thread(target=happy_multiply, args=(10,2))
    thread2 = threading.Thread(target=happy_divide, args=(10,2))
    # Start threads..
    thread1.start()
    thread1.join() # ..and make sure thread 1 is fully executed
    thread2.start() # before we start thread 2
    thread2.join()
    print("All done!")
```

We create two functions in Listing 6-11, namely, *happy_multiply* and *happy_divide*. These take two arguments each. With the former, we multiply *num* with *num2*, while the latter divides *num* by *num2*. The results are then simply printed on screen.

Now, there's one function in Listing 6-11 you should pay close attention to; Python's *join()* method is there to make sure a thread has done its processing fully before moving on with a listing. If you were to remove the line *thread1. join()*, the output of Listing 6-4 would be a jumbled mess.

A *race condition* in the context of concurrent processing refers to a scenario in which two or more processes are modifying a resource, such as a file, simultaneously. The end result depends on which process gets there first. This is considered an undesirable scenario.

# Implementing Multiprocessing in Python

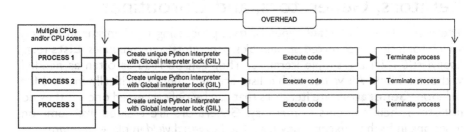

**Figure 6-2.** A partial visualization of multiprocessing in Python using three processes

Although the approach of multiprocessing produces highly CPU-efficient code in general, minor issues of overhead may still occur. If a multiprocessing project in Python has these issues, they typically take place during the initialization or termination of a process (see Figure 6-2).

Now, for a simple demonstration of Python's multiprocessing module, see Listing 6-12.

**Listing 6-12.** *A listing in Python demonstrating elementary use of the multiprocessing module*

```python
import time
import multiprocessing

def counter(): # Define a function, counter()
    name = multiprocessing.current_process().name
    print (name, "appears!")

    for i in range(3):
        time.sleep(1) # Delay for one second for dramatic effect
        print (name, i+1,"/ 3")

if __name__ == '__main__': # Define this listing as "main", the one to execute
    counter1 = multiprocessing.Process(name='Counter A', target=counter)
    counter2 = multiprocessing.Process(name='Counter B', target=counter)
    counter3 = multiprocessing.Process(target=counter) # No name given..
```

```
counter1.start()
counter2.start()
counter3.start() # This nameless counter simply outputs "Process-3"
```

Each process in Python has a name variable as is evident from Listing 6-12. If none is defined, a generic label of *Process-[process number]* will be automatically assigned.

# Iterators, Generators, and Coroutines

There are three important types of data-processing mechanisms in Python which sometimes get mixed up: *iterables, generators,* and *coroutines*. **Lists** (e.g., *happyList[0,1,2]*) are simple iterables. They can be read as often as needed without a hitch. All values within lists are kept until specifically marked for deletion. **Generators** are iterators that can be only accessed once as they do not store their contents in memory. Generators are created like common functions in Python except they have the keyword *yield* in place of *return*.

---

Generators are useful when reading the attributes of large files, such as their row counts. Generators put to this use will yield the data that's not up to date and thus not needed, avoiding memory errors and making Python programs run more efficiently.

---

**Coroutines** are a unique type of function that can yield control over to a calling function without ending their context in the process; coroutines maintain their idle state smoothly in the background. In other words, they are used for cooperative multitasking.

# Asyncio: The Odd One Out?

Asyncio, short for *asynchronous input/output,* is a module in Python designed for writing concurrently running code. Despite having similarities with both threading and multiprocessing, it actually represents a different approach, referred to as *cooperative multitasking*. The asyncio module offers a kind of pseudo-concurrency using a single process running in a single thread.

And what does it mean to work with asynchronous code in Python? Well, code written with this approach can be safely paused in order for other code snippets within a project to execute their tasks. An asynchronous process offers its downtime for other processes to run their course; this is how a type of concurrency can indeed be attained with the asyncio module.

# The Asynchronous Event Loop

The main component of an asynchronous Python project is the *event loop;* we run our subprocesses from this construct. Tasks are scheduled in an event loop and managed by a thread. Basically, the event loop is there to coordinate tasks and make sure everything runs smoothly when we're working with the asyncio module. Let's see how to actually implement the asyncio module with Listing 6-13.

***Listing 6-13.*** *A listing in Python demonstrating asynchronous chained coroutines and the use of an event loop*

```python
import asyncio

async def prime_number_checker(x): # Define a function which takes x as input
    # Go to sleep for one second, potentially letting other functions
    # do their thing while we're asleep
    await asyncio.sleep(1.0)
    message1 = "%d isn't a prime number.." % x # Set default message

    if x > 1:
        for i in range(2, x):
            # Apply the modulo-operator (%) on variable x.
            # If the ensuing remainder does not equal zero, update "message1"
            if (x % i) != 0:
                message1 = "%d is a prime number!" % x
                break # Break out of the loop
        return message1

async def print_result(y): # Define a function which takes y as input
    result = await prime_number_checker(y) # Await for other function to finish
    print(result) # Print results from function prime_number_checker()
happyloop = asyncio.get_event_loop()
# See if 2, 11, and 15 are prime numbers
happyloop.run_until_complete(print_result(2))
happyloop.run_until_complete(print_result(11))
happyloop.run_until_complete(print_result(15))
happyloop.close()
```

In Listing 6-13, we are looking for prime numbers (i.e., numbers that have only two factors: themselves and 1). We define two asynchronous functions/coroutines, *prime_number_checker(x)* and *print_result(y)*, both of them with the keywords *async def* as that's how it's done with the asyncio module.

Now, the first function we defined begins with the line *await asyncio.sleep(1.0)*. Compared to the regular sleep method in Python, this asynchronous variety doesn't freeze the program; instead, it gives a specified time period for other tasks to complete in the background.

The line *result = await prime_number_checker(y)* in the second coroutine is there to make sure the first function has completed its execution. *Await* is indeed a somewhat self-explanatory and crucial keyword in the asynchronous approach.

To get our asynchronous listing fully running, we need to work with the event loop. We do this by creating a new loop object, *happyloop*, and summoning a function called *asyncio.get_event_loop()*. Although there are several varieties of functions for event loop management, for the sake of clarity, we'll only cover the aforementioned approach in this example.

Next, in Listing 6-13, the function *run_until_complete* actually executes our *print_result(y)* function until its respective tasks are fully completed. Finally, we end our event loop by summoning the close method.

## Concurrency in Python: A Recap

It's possible to get confused by all of the processing approaches Python offers. Let's therefore end the chapter with a recap on some of the core concepts involved (see Table 6-7).

**Table 6-7.** The main approaches of concurrent programming in Python

| | | |
|---|---|---|
| **Multiprocessing** | Runs multiple processes simultaneously; a separate Python interpreter with global interpreter lock (GIL) is created for each process | Can utilize multiple CPUs and/or CPU cores in a system |
| **Multithreading** | Scheduled task execution prioritized by the operating system. Limited by a single GIL | Also called *preemptive multitasking*. Runs on a single CPU/core |
| **Asynchronous processing** | Scheduling decided on by tasks Limited by a single GIL | Also called *cooperative multitasking*. Runs on a single CPU/core. Introduced in Python version 3.0 |

# Python Lambda Functions

Think of a *lambda function* as a disposable function. Lambda functions are nameless and often small scale in nature. Their syntax is simply as follows:

- *lambda (arguments) : (expressions)*

Here's a simple lambda function: *sum1 = lambda x, y : x + y*. For a slightly more complex example, see Listing 6-14.

*Listing 6-14.* *A listing demonstrating lambda functions in Python*

```
def happymultiply(b):
  return lambda a : a * b

result1 = happymultiply(5)
result2 = happymultiply(10)
result3 = happymultiply(50)

print("Result 1:", result1(6))
print("Result 2:", result2(6))
print("Result 3:", result3(6))
```

Now, there are three methods in Python which work exceptionally well with lambda functions: *map( )*, *filter( )*, and *reduce( )*. Filter( ) takes a list and creates a new one consisting of all elements which return true. Map( ) also creates a new list out of iterables it processes; think of it as a loop-free iterator function. Finally, we have reduce( ) which applies a function to a list (or other iterables) and returns a single value, again sometimes freeing us from the use of loops altogether (see Listing 6-15).

*Listing 6-15.* *A listing with a lambda function applied on a filtered list in Python*

```
from functools import reduce # Import code module needed for reduce()

# Create a list containing seven values
middle_aged = [6, 120, 65, 40, 55, 57, 45]
# Display list before manipulations
print("Ages of all people in the study:", middle_aged)

# Filter list for ages between 40 and 59
middle_aged = list(filter(lambda age: age>=40 and age<60, middle_aged))
print("Middle aged people:", middle_aged)

# Summon map() and double the values in the list "middle_aged"
elderly = list(map(lambda x: x * 2, middle_aged))
print("They will live to:", elderly)
```

```
# Summon reduce() to add all elements in "middle_aged" together
total_years = reduce(lambda x, y: x + y, middle_aged)
print("Their combined time spent alive so far:", total_years, "years")
```

## Zipping in Python

Named after the zipper, the renowned clothing closure mechanism, a *zip* in Python refers to a method of combining the elements of two or more iterables. Zipping is a great tool when creating dictionary data structures in Python, for one. And no, this variety of zip doesn't have anything to do with the popular archiving file format, ZIP, which we'll review later in this chapter.

Now, a zip function in Python takes two iterables (e.g., lists) and returns a set of tuples (see Listing 6-16).

***Listing 6-16.*** *A listing in Python demonstrating the zip function*

```
# Define two lists
letters1 = ['z', 'a', 'r', 'd', 'o', 'z']
numbers1 = [1, 2, 3, 4, 5, 6]

# Create zip object, zip1, using "letters1" and "numbers1"
zip1 = zip(letters1, numbers1)

for i in zip1: # Display zip contents
    print(i)
# Define new list, "letters2"
letters2 = ['Z', 'A', 'R', 'D', 'O', 'Z']

# Create second zip object, zip2, using "letters1", "numbers1", and "letters2"
zip2 = zip(letters2, numbers1, letters1)

for i in zip2: # Display second zip contents
    print(i)
```

## More on Zipping

There are a number of scenarios in which basic zipping just won't cut it. One of them involves zips with incomplete tuples. Luckily, we have a method called *zip_longest*. Found in the code module *itertools*, this method fills in any missing elements with the placeholder data of your choosing, no less. See Listing 6-17 for a demonstration.

**Listing 6-17.** *A listing in Python demonstrating the zip_longest method*

```python
from itertools import zip_longest
letterlist = ['a', 'b', 'c']
numberlist = [1, 2, 3, 4]
maximum = range(5) # Define zip length and store it into "maximum"
# Summon zip_longest()
zipped1 = zip_longest(numberlist, letterlist, maximum, fillvalue='blank')
# Display zip contents
for i in zipped1:
    print(i)
```

You may wonder if a zipper in Python can be unzipped. The answer is a resounding yes (see Listing 6-18).

**Listing 6-18.** *A listing in Python demonstrating unzipping.*

```python
letters = ['A', 'B', 'C', 'D']
numbers = [1, 2, 3, 4]

zipped1 = zip(letters, numbers) # Zip the data
zipped_data = list(zipped1)
print("Here's the zip:", zipped_data)

a, b = zip(*zipped_data) # Unzip the data using the asterisk-operator
print("Next comes the data, unzipped!")
print('Letters:', a)
print('Numbers:', b)
```

# Working with the Other ZIP

As previously mentioned in this chapter, *zip* is a word with at least two popular meanings in the context of computing. We explored zipping (and unzipping) in Python, covering the first meaning. Now it's time to work with the other ZIP, the popular archive file format, from within any Python IDE.

Now, directories (and their subdirectories) compressed with ZIP software end up as a single file which also tends to be considerably smaller in size than its uncompressed contents. This is obviously a great solution for network-based file delivery. Naturally, there are several file compression solutions available, but as of 2021, ZIP is still a fantastically ubiquitous file archive format, available for all popular operating systems.

---

ZIP was created by *Phil Katz* and *Gary Conway* back in 1989. The ZIP compression technology has been more recently used as the basis for the *Java Archive (JAR)* file format—and many others.

---

Python, too, likes its ZIP files. We can actually operate them from within a Python IDE. There's a code module for it aptly called *zipfile*. See Listing 6-19 for a demonstration on how to create a ZIP file and how to display its contents in Python.

**Listing 6-19.** *A listing demonstrating the use of ZIP file archives from inside Python*

```python
import os
from os.path import basename
from zipfile import ZipFile # Include ZipFile module

lookfor = "thread" # Create a variable for the string we plan to look for
# Define a new function, make_a_zip
def make_a_zip(dirName, zipFileName, filter):
    # Create a new ZipFile-object with attribute w for (over)writing
    with ZipFile(zipFileName, 'w') as zip_object1:
        # Start iteration of files in the directory specified
        for folderName, subfolders, filenames in os.walk(dirName):
            for file in filenames:
                if filter(file):
                    # Create full file-path
                    filePath = os.path.join(folderName, file)
                    # Add file to zip using write() method
                    zip_object1.write(filePath, basename(filePath))
# Summon make_a_zip() and give it the current directory to work with
# Also only look for filenames with the string "thread" in them
make_a_zip('..', 'happy.zip', lambda name: lookfor in name)
print("All files containing <<", lookfor, ">> in their name are now inside
happy.zip!")
# Create a ZipFile Object and load happy.zip into it (using attribute r for
reading)
with ZipFile('happy.zip', 'r') as zip_object2:
    # Summon namelist() and store contents in "file_in_zip" variable
    files_in_zip = zip_object2.namelist()
    # Iterate through files_in_zip and print each element
    print("\nThese files were stored in happy.zip:")
    for i in files_in_zip:
        print(i)
```

In Listing 6-19, you'll see two major mechanics of Python's ZIP support at play: making a new file archive (i.e., *happy.zip*) and retrieving the names of the files stored inside it. The example also shows you how to use wildcard-based functionality when gathering files to an archive. In this case, we'll only look for files with the string "thread" somewhere in their file name.

The *with* statements used in tandem with a *ZipFile* are basically there to provide clarity into our listing. For one, they're freeing us from using closing methods (e.g., *happyfile.close( )*) which are usually needed after operations on a file are completed.

---

Listing 6-19 will execute in your current Python directory, so your results may vary.

---

We'll return to the intricacies of the Python-language later in the book.

# In Closing

Finishing this chapter, you'll have hopefully learned the following:

- How to open, create, and delete files with Python

- Basic directory management in Python

- What regular expressions (RegEx) refer to

- How and when to summon match( ), search( ), and fullmatch( ) for RegEx work

- How to implement multithreading and multiprocessing in Python and what their main differences are

- What the global interpreter lock (GIL) refers to

- The basics of asynchronous programming in Python using *asyncio*

- What lambda functions are useful for

- The basics of zipping and working with ZIP file archives in Python

Chapter 7 will see us exploring the more advanced side of the sturdy and popular C# language.

# Calendars, Culture, and Multithreading in C#

This chapter is dedicated to one of the most versatile languages out there: the mighty C#. By now, you are hopefully familiar with the basic syntax of this language and the setting up of an integrated development environment. We'll hereby proceed to explore some of the more advanced topics related to this stout language, including the basics of calendar work and multithreading.

## Dates in C#

Like Java and Python, C# offers all you need when it comes to working with dates and calendars. Let's peek at a program in where we access dates and calendars, shall we? (See Listing 7-1.)

© Robert Ciesla 2021

R. Ciesla, *Programming Basics*, https://doi.org/10.1007/978-1-4842-7286-2_7

*Listing 7-1.* A listing in C# demonstrating the use of DateTime objects (the date in question is recording artist Rick Astley's date of birth)

```
using System;
public class Example
{
    public static void Main()
    { // Create a new DateTime-object, "happydate"
        DateTime happydate = new DateTime(1966, 2, 6, 5, 20, 0);
        // Display object data
        Console.WriteLine("Our special date is {0}", happydate.ToString());
        // Fetch and display year and day of the week for our date-object
        Console.WriteLine("Back  in  {0}  it  was  {1}!",  happydate.Year,
        happydate.DayOfWeek);
        // Create a second DateTime-object
            DateTime happydate2 = DateTime.Now;
            Console.WriteLine("As  for  right  now,  it's  a  {1}  in  {0}!",
            happydate2.Year, happydate2.DayOfWeek);
    }
}
```

We start Listing 7-1 off by creating an object we chose to call *happydate*. It shall be an instance of the C# DateTime structure and use a specific constructor for setting the year, month, and time of day. We then display this date using a *Console.WriteLine* with a *{0}* formatting mark inside for including the first, and in this case only, parameter. The happydate object is also converted into currently active *cultural-specific formatting conventions* using the ToString method.

---

The DateTime structures are a part of the System namespace in C#, so they don't need to be included in our projects using any other way.

---

The DateTime structure in C# includes a plethora of properties for accessing calendar-related data from year down to millisecond. See Table 7-1 for a rundown.

*Table 7-1.* Some core properties included in the DateTime structure in C#

| Now | Day | Millisecond |
|-----|-----|-------------|
| Date | Hour | TimeOfDay |
| Year | Minute | DayOfWeek |
| Month | Second | DayOfYear |

# The System.Globalization Namespace

Global culture is a concept taken quite seriously by C#. *Globalization* refers to designing an application for users from any part of the globe. *Localization* refers to the process of tailoring an application to conform to the requirements of a specific culture. In practice, these concepts deal with the different calendars, currencies, languages, and locations our planet offers. In C#, we have a large number of methods and properties for presenting localized information with. A lot of them originate in the *System.Globalization* namespace.

# Working with World Calendars

The Calendar class in C# includes a total of 14 different calendars for your localization needs. See Table 7-2 to glance at eight of them.

**Table 7-2.** Some calendars included in C#

| | | | |
|---|---|---|---|
| GregorianCalendar | Most widely used calendar in the world | JulianCalendar | In use by the Russian Orthodox church |
| HebrewCalendar | Official calendar of Israel. Also called the Jewish calendar | PersianCalendar | Official calendar of Iran and Afghanistan |
| HijriCalendar | Also called the Islamic calendar | ThaiBuddhistCalendar | Used in Thailand. Is set 543 years ahead of the Gregorian calendar |
| JapaneseCalendar | Similar to the Gregorian calendar, adds year designations based on the year of the reign of the current emperor of Japan | UmAlQuraCalendar | Used in Saudi Arabia, similar to the Hijri |

In Listing 7-2, you'll find a program which takes a date set in the Gregorian calendar (i.e., the 31st of December 2021) and converts that into four other calendars. We'll access relevant date-related data using methods like GetYear() and GetMonth(). We also specify a custom formatting pattern for our Gregorian DateTime object using a ToString method.

**Listing 7-2.** *A listing demonstrating displaying information using five different calendars in C#*

```
using System;
using System.Globalization;
public class CalendarsExample
{
    public static void Main()
    {
            // Create a new Gregorian DateTime-object, date1
            DateTime date1 = new DateTime(2021, 12, 31, new GregorianCalendar());
            // Create four more objects for the four other types of calendars
            JapaneseCalendar japanese = new JapaneseCalendar();
            PersianCalendar persian = new PersianCalendar();
            HijriCalendar hijri = new HijriCalendar();
            ThaiBuddhistCalendar thai = new ThaiBuddhistCalendar();
Console.WriteLine("When the Gregorian Calendar says it's {0}..", date1.
ToString("dd.MM.yyyy"));
Console.WriteLine("> The Japanese Calendar says it's year {0}.", japanese.
GetYear(date1));
Console.WriteLine("> The Persian Calendar says it's the year {0} and the
{1}th month of the year.", persian.GetYear(date1), persian.GetMonth(date1));
Console.WriteLine("> The Hijri Calendar says it's the year {0} and it's {1}.",
hijri.GetYear(date1), hijri.GetDayOfWeek(date1));
Console.WriteLine("> The Thai Buddhist Calendar says it's the year {0} and the
{1}th month of the year.", thai.GetYear(date1), thai.GetMonth(date1));
    }
}
```

# The CultureInfo Class

The CultureInfo class provides us with the means of localizing our programs in C#. This includes displaying time, calendar, and currency information tailored to specific locales. To grant us access to the CultureInfo class, we'll need to have our program again use the namespace *System.Globalization*.

C# uses *language-culture codes* for its localization. In the listing to follow, we used four, that is, *en-US*, *fi-FI*, *se-SE*, and *es-ES*. The first two letters in this code represent a language, while the second, capitalized pair of letters refer to a specific region. For example, the German language (*de*) can be represented with additional culture codes, for example, *de-AT* (Austria), *de-CH* (Switzerland), and *de-LI* (Lichtenstein). Now, see Listing 7-3 for a demonstration.

---

The language-culture codes in C# are based on the *ISO 3166-1 Country list.* A total of 249 language-culture codes are supported as of 2021.

---

*Listing 7-3.* *A listing demonstrating the use of localization in C# using the CultureInfo class*

```csharp
using System;
using System.Globalization;
public class CultureInfoExample
{
    public static void Main()
    {
        // Create an array of four CultureInfo-objects called "jollycultures"
        CultureInfo[] jollycultures = new CultureInfo[] {
        new CultureInfo("en-US"), // US
        new CultureInfo("fi-FI"), // Finnish
        new CultureInfo("se-SE"), // Sami in Northern Sweden
        new CultureInfo("es-ES")}; // Spanish
// Create a new DateTime-object, "date1", assigning calendar-information into it
DateTime date1 = new DateTime(1952, 12, 1, 15, 30, 00);
// Display unformatted date
Console.WriteLine("The special date is " + date1 + " in your current
locale.\n");
// Use the foreach-keyword to loop through all of the jollycultures-objects
// and display their contents, using "i" as a temporary iterator-variable
        foreach (CultureInfo i in jollycultures)
        {
                Console.WriteLine("This date in {0} is.. {1} ({2})", i.EnglishName,
                date1.ToString(i), i.Name);
        }
    }
}
```

In Listing 7-3, we created four instances of class CultureInfo to demonstrate the locales of the United States, Finland, Sami (in Northern Sweden), and Spain as they pertain to C#.

We went with the solution to use a *foreach* element when displaying CultureInfo objects. A *foreach* in C# is an alternative to the for-loop and one that tends to be better suited when iterating through arrays. This element works beautifully with instances of CultureInfo, for one.

Now it's time for a small example of currency formatting (see Listing 7-4).

*Listing 7-4.* *A listing demonstrating currency formats in the C# CultureInfo class*

```csharp
using System.Globalization;
public class JollyCurrencies
{
    public static void Main()
    {
```

```
        int cash = 10000;
                // Display cash amount without currency-format
                Console.WriteLine("No currency-format: " + cash.ToString());
                // Set CurrentCulture to Finnish in Finland.
                Thread.CurrentThread.CurrentCulture = new CultureInfo("fi-FI");
                // Add the appropriate currency-format using "c"
                Console.WriteLine("Finnish currency-format: " + cash.
                ToString("c"));
                // Set CurrentCulture to Belarusian in Belarus and display string
        Thread.CurrentThread.CurrentCulture = new CultureInfo("be-BY");
        Console.WriteLine("Belarusian currency-format: " + cash.ToString("c"));
                // Set CurrentCulture to Chinese in People's Republic of China
        Thread.CurrentThread.CurrentCulture = new CultureInfo("zh-CN");
        Console.WriteLine("Chinese currency-format: " + cash.ToString("c"));
                }
}
```

In Listing 7-4, we create and display three different currency formats for Finnish, Belarusian, and Chinese languages, respectively. The method *ToString("c")* is there to designate a currency.

# The File Class in C#

C# offers versatile facilities for all types of file manipulation through a class simply called *File*. We can read and display text files, create new ones, and retrieve numerous types of attributes such as creation date—and much more.

In Listing 7-5, we create a new file from within C# we'll call *apress.txt*. Inside it, we'll write a little message ("Apress is the best publisher!"). Not stopping there, we'll proceed to read and display the contents of the file we just created.

To use the File class, we need the System.IO namespace in our program.

***Listing 7-5.*** *A listing demonstrating the TextWriter and TextReader classes in C#*

```
using System;
using System.IO;
class HappyTextWriter
{
    static void Main(string[] args)
    {
    using (TextWriter happywriter = File.CreateText("c:\\apress.txt"))
            {
                happywriter.WriteLine("Apress is the best publisher!");
            }
    Console.WriteLine("Textfile created in C:\n\nIt reads:");
    // Open the file we just created and display its contents
```

```
using (TextReader happyreader1 = File.OpenText("c:\\apress.txt"))
        {
            Console.WriteLine(happyreader1.ReadToEnd());
        }
    }
}
```

Text files aside, there is another file format for us to work with. In Listing 7-6, we'll work with this other main type: *binary files*. This format is very versatile and can store text, numbers, and basically anything we could ever use. In the next listing, we'll be creating a binary file and storing a floating-point number, a string of text, and a boolean variable into it. Again, we need to leverage the File class using the System.IO namespace.

**Listing 7-6.** *A listing demonstrating the BinaryWriter and BinaryReader classes in C#*

```
using System;
using System.IO;
class JollyBinaryTest {
            static void Main(string[] args)
        {
        string filename1 = "c:\\binarystuff.dat"; // Define  our  path  and
                                                              filename
/* Create a new BinaryWriter-object (writer1) and save three lines/types
of  information into it */
using (BinaryWriter writer1 = new BinaryWriter(File.Open(filename1, FileMode.
Create)))
{
writer1.Write(55.52F);  // Write a floating point number
writer1.Write("Oranges are great"); // Write a string
writer1.Write(true); // Write a boolean (true/false) variable
}
Console.WriteLine("Data written into binary file " + filename1 + "!\n");
/* Create a new BinaryReader-object (reader1) and use it to decipher the
   binary data in our file using the appropriate methods, e.g. ReadSingle()
   for the floating point */
using (BinaryReader reader1 = new BinaryReader(File.Open(filename1,
FileMode.Open)))
{
Console.WriteLine("First line: " + reader1.ReadSingle() ); // Read a floating
                                                                    point
Console.WriteLine("Second line: " + reader1.ReadString() ); // Read a string
Console.WriteLine("Third line: " + reader1.ReadBoolean() ); // Read a boolean
                                                                   variable
}
}
}
```

---

When working with nonspecific binary files, it's somewhat customary to use the file extension *.dat*—as in data.

---

# The FileInfo Class

The File class has an alternative in C#; *FileInfo* offers more control and is more useful under certain conditions. Let's take a peek at how to access file attributes with FileInfo with Listing 7-7.

*Listing 7-7.  A listing demonstrating file-attribute access using the C# FileInfo class*

```
using System;
using System.IO;
class FileInfoAttributeFun
{
public static void Main()
{
            string fileName1 = @"C:\apress.txt"; // Set our target file
            FileInfo ourfile = new FileInfo(fileName1);
            string na = ourfile.FullName;
    Console.WriteLine("Attributes for " + na + ":");
            string ex = ourfile.Extension;
    Console.WriteLine("File extension: " + ex);
            bool ro = ourfile.IsReadOnly;
            Console.WriteLine("Read-only file: " + ro);
            long sz = ourfile.Length;
    Console.WriteLine("Size: " + sz + " bytes");
            DateTime ct = ourfile.CreationTime;
    Console.WriteLine("Creation time: " + ct);
            DateTime la = ourfile.LastAccessTime;
            Console.WriteLine("Last access: " + la);
    }
}
```

Listing 7-7 expects you to have a text file, *apress.txt*, in the root directory of your Windows hard drive. You can modify *filename1* to point at a different location and/or a different text file to make Listing 7-7 work its magic.

Now would be a good time to take a peek at some of the most commonly used attributes accessible by the FileInfo. See Table 7-3 for a rundown.

**Table 7-3.** Some properties included in the FileInfo class in C#.

| Name | Returns a file's name | Exists | Is used to determine if a specific file exists |
|------|----------------------|--------|-----------------------------------------------|
| Fullname | Returns a file's full name and directory path (e.g., C:\MyFolder\myfile.txt) | Length | Returns a file's size in bytes |
| CreationTime | Returns or changes a file's "date of birth" | Directory | Returns an instance of the parent directory |
| LastAccessTime | Returns or changes the time of last access of a file or directory | Attributes | Returns or changes a file's attributes |

Let's next look at a somewhat more thorough example of C# file operations. In Listing 7-8, we use the FileInfo class somewhat more extensively. This includes copying a file using the CopyTo method as well as file removal using the Delete method.

**Listing 7-8.** *A listing in C# demonstrating some file operations found in the FileInfo class*

```
using System;
using System.IO;
class FileInfoExample
{
public static void Main()
{
string filename1 = @"C:\wackyfile.txt"; // Path to main file
string file2 = @"c:\wacky_copy.txt"; // Path to copy of main file
FileInfo ourfile = new FileInfo(filename1); // Create new FileInfo-object,
                                            "ourfile"
FileInfo ourfile_copy = new FileInfo(file2); // Do the same for "ourfile_copy"
            // Use Exists-property to determine if file has already been
               created
            if(!ourfile.Exists) {
            File.Create(filename1).Dispose(); // Create file and disable
                                              file-lock on "ourfile"
            Console.WriteLine("File not found. Creating " + filename1);
            } else Console.WriteLine("File found.");
            // Display full name of our file
            Console.WriteLine("Attempting to make a copy of " + ourfile.
            FullName);
            // See if copy exists. If it doesn't, duplicate file
            if(!ourfile_copy.Exists) { ourfile.CopyTo(file2);
            Console.WriteLine("{0} has been copied as {1}", ourfile, file2);
            } else Console.WriteLine("File not copied. Duplicate already
            found.");
            // Prompt user for input
```

```
Console.WriteLine("Would you like to delete these files? (y/n)");
char input1 = (char)Console.Read(); // Assign a Console.Read()
                                          to character "input1"
if(input1=='y') { // If user inputs 'y' delete both files
Console.WriteLine("Deleting files..");
ourfile.Delete();
ourfile_copy.Delete();
} else Console.WriteLine("Files in C:\\ not deleted.");
    }
}
```

Let's go through Listing 7-8 in detail. First, we define two strings: *filename1* and *file2*. These strings contain full file paths and point to two files in the Windows root directory C:. We could also simply leave the paths out and stick with the file name only (i.e., *wackyfile.txt* and *wacky_copy.txt*).

Next, we create an object using the FileInfo class, calling it *ourfile*. Another object, *ourfile_copy*, is then created for the file duplicate. We needed to instantiate FileInfo in order to use the class methods later on.

---

The at sign, that is, @, before a string value indicates a literal string in C#. This means the strings which follow will not be parsed for any escape sequences, such as "\\" for a backslash. Compare the following lines (the top one being the literal string):

```
string file1 = @"c:\user\xerxes\documents\text\nincompoop.txt";

string file1 = "c:\\user\\xerxes\\documents\\text\\nincompoop.txt";
```

---

The line *if(!ourfile.Exists)* is there to examine the rather self-explanatory Exists property of object ourfile. With an exclamation mark in front of it, the conditional clause reads "if ourfile does NOT exist." Moving on, the line *File. Create(filename1).Dispose();* contains two instructions. First, the Create method is there to make an actual file on your storage system. The Dispose method basically releases the file's access status. Without it, we may run into issues later in the program when manipulating this file.

Now, back to our conditional clause. It ends with the keyword *else*, reading "if ourfile DOES exist," and in this scenario, it outputs the message "File found." Next, we attempt to copy the object *ourfile*. It's time for another conditional clause. The line *if(!ourfile_copy.Exists) { ourfile.CopyTo(file2);* is there to again examine the existence of a file, this time focusing on the other file we defined earlier, *ourfile_copy*. If it does not exist, we summon the CopyTo method to copy ourfile (i.e., *wackyfile.txt*) onto file2 (i.e., *wacky_copy.txt*). We again have an optional else keyword at the end of our conditional clause. This time it's there to display the message "File not found. Duplicate already found."

We now move on to some user interaction. The user is prompted to press "y" (and hit return) if they wish to delete both the original file and its duplicate. This is achieved with the Delete method. Should the user enter any other character instead of "y," the files remain intact and a message stating "Files in C:\ not deleted." is displayed instead.

# File vs. FileInfo: What's the Difference?

The File and FileInfo classes of C# are quite similar. However, there are reasons for why they remain separate entities in the language. The FileInfo class is preferable when multiple operations on a file are needed, while File works best for single operations. FileInfo also offers a touch more manual control with its byte-sized file manipulations.

The methods inside File are static, whereas those inside FileInfo are instance based. Static methods take more arguments, such as full directory paths. In turn, under specific scenarios, such as coding for network-based environments, the somewhat more arduous File class might actually yield more effective results (see Table 7-4).

**Table 7-4.** The main differences between File and FileInfo classes in C#

| File | FileInfo |
|---|---|
| Uses static methods | Uses instance-based methods |
| Does not need to be instantiated | Needs to be instantiated |
| Offers more methods | Offers fewer methods |
| May offer faster performance under some scenarios, e.g., with network traffic | Has finer control over file reading and writing operations |

To observe some manual control provided by FileInfo, see Listing 7-9.

**Listing 7-9.** *A listing demonstrating manual control for reading data using FileInfo and FileStream classes in C#*

```
using System;
using System.IO;
// Create a new FileInfo object, "fileobj1"
FileInfo fileobj1 = new FileInfo(@"c:\apress.txt"); // This text-file should
                                          contain something
// Open the file for reading: this line works with FileInfo only; not with File
FileStream filestream1 = fileobj1.Open(FileMode.Open, FileAccess.Read);
// Create a byte array sharing the length of our filestream
byte[] bytearray1 = new byte[filestream1.Length];
```

```
// Set variable for a byte-counter and feed the length of our file into it
int howmanybytes = (int)bytearray1.Length;
int bytesread = 0;
// Read our file, a byte at a time using a while-loop
while (howmanybytes > 0)
{
    int i = filestream1.Read(bytearray1, bytesread, howmanybytes);
    if (i == 0) break; // Once we have zero bytes left, break loop
    howmanybytes-=i;
        bytesread+=i;
}
// Convert bytes into string which uses UTF-8 character encoding
string string1 = Encoding.UTF8.GetString(bytearray1);
Console.WriteLine(string1); // Display string
```

The FileStream class allows us to read and write files on a byte-by-byte basis. This is done using the Open method in Listing 7-9. This is a versatile method which takes several attributes; to open our file in a read-only mode, we enter the arguments FileMode.Open and FileAccess.Read into the Open method. Next in the listing, we create a byte array, using the keyword byte[ ]. As a reminder, an array is a collection of values; they might consist of numbers, characters, strings, or bytes. In C#, arrays are defined using square brackets (as a second reminder, bytes consist of eight bits each and are used frequently to denote alphabetical characters, for one).

Next up, with the line int howmanybytes = (int)bytearray1.Length; we create an integer, howmanybytes, into which we apply a Length method in order to find out our file's size in bytes. In the ensuing while loop, bytes are read using the Read method.

To be more precise, this while loop is to be executed while the variable howmanybytes remains greater than zero. The file stream we defined earlier, filestream1, has the Read method applied on it with the byte array (bytearray1), the amount of bytes read so far (bytesread), and the total amount of bytes to be read (howmanybytes) as the method's arguments. This output is fed into variable i. We break out of this loop when i reaches zero using the break keyword.

The final steps of Listing 7-9 consist of first converting bytearray1 into readable Unicode characters and storing it into string1 after which this string is then displayed.

---

Using *UTF-8* character encoding, each Latin alphanumerical character stored in a string typically occupies two bytes, that is, 16 bits.

---

# Garbage Collection in C#

The concept of *garbage collection (GC)* basically refers to automated memory management. This mechanism is there to allocate and free RAM as needed by a program; programming languages with support for garbage collection free the programmer from these tasks. Most modern languages, including C#, support GC out of the box. This feature can also be added into languages without native support in the form of additional software libraries.

As a programming project grows, it usually includes more and more variables and other data structures which eat up RAM unless properly taken care of. Managing these resources can become a bit of a pest for the programmer. Also, compromised memory allocation can cause stability issues.

Now, garbage collection in C# is invoked under the following three scenarios:

1.  Your computer is running low on physical memory. The more RAM your system has, the less frequently this is going to take place.

2.  A specific threshold for memory that's used by allocated objects is surpassed. This threshold is updated in real time by the garbage collection components.

3.  A *GC.Collect* method is summoned by the programmer(s). This is rarely necessary for smaller projects.

# Native vs. Managed Heap

The *native heap* is dynamically allocated memory managed by the operating system. Native heap memory is allocated and de-allocated on the fly whenever a program is executed. The area of memory referred to as the *managed heap* is a different entity. Every separate process gets its own managed heap. All threads inside a process also share this memory space.

# Multithreading in C#

Like you may have expected, multithreading is indeed well and truly supported in C#. See Listing 7-10 for a demonstration. First, we define a custom method, *ChildThread()*, to give birth to new threads. We are to later create three threads which are to simultaneously use the Sleep method, which simply pause a thread's processing. Inside our threads, these methods are assigned a random value between 0 and 6000 milliseconds for a maximum of 6 seconds of delay, all to be counted simultaneously as per the thread-based paradigm.

Programs consist of *processes*. *Threads* are the entities inside processes which can be scheduled whenever they're most needed. In C#, too, we can exert a lot of control over the creation and other life cycle events of threads.

Next in our custom method, we retrieve a rather long-winded property called *System.Threading.Thread.CurrentThread.ManagedThreadId* for a unique identification number for each running thread, storing it into *happyID*.

When setting up thread information, the variable *delay* is divided by a thousand (i.e., multiplied by 0.001) for displaying it in seconds. We also utilize the Round method from the C# Math class to round our delay integer to two decimals.

**Listing 7-10.** *A listing demonstrating how child threads are created in C#*

```
using System;
using System.Threading;
public static void ChildThread() {
Random randomnr = new Random(); // Create a new Random-object, "randomnr"
int delay = randomnr.Next(0, 6000); // Set a random delay between zero and six
seconds using our random-object
/* Assign thread ID number, i.e.   System.Threading.Thread.CurrentThread.
ManagedThreadId, into integer "happyID" */
int happyID = System.Threading.Thread.CurrentThread.ManagedThreadId;
        Console.WriteLine("Happy thread " + happyID + " starts!");
        // Round delay amount to two decimals when displaying it
        Console.WriteLine("Happy thread " + happyID + " is paused for {0}
        seconds..", Math.Round(delay * 0.001, 2) );
        Thread.Sleep(delay);
        Console.WriteLine("Happy thread " + happyID + " will now resume!");
    }

    static void Main(string[] args) {
        ThreadStart child = new ThreadStart(ChildThread);
        for(int i=0; i<3; ++i) { // Create a total of three child-threads
        Thread childThread = new Thread(child);
        childThread.Start(); // Commence execution of thread
    }
}
```

The main method of Listing 7-10 is rather simple. Using a for-loop, we create exactly three instances of ChildThread, commencing their execution using the *Start()* method found in the C# Thread-class.

# Locks and Attributes in C# Threads

Like Java and Python, C# offers a locking mechanism for its threaded applications. With locks, we can make our threads synchronized (see Listing 7-11).

*Listing 7-11.* A listing in C# demonstrating thread locking and accessing some thread properties

```csharp
using System;
using System.Threading;
    public class LockingThreads
    {
        public void OurThread()
        {
            // Get a handle for the currently executing thread
            // so we can retrieve its properties, such as Name
            Thread wackyhandle = Thread.CurrentThread;
            // Apply a lock to synchronize thread
            lock(this) { // Locked code begins
            Console.WriteLine("(This thread is "+wackyhandle.ThreadState+"
            with " + wackyhandle.Priority + " priority)");
                for(int i=0; i<3; ++i) {
Console.WriteLine(wackyhandle.Name + " has been working for " +i+ " hours");
        Thread.Sleep(400); // Wait for 0.4 seconds before next line
        }
        } // Locked code ends
    }
}
    public static void Main()
    {
    LockingThreads jollythread = new LockingThreads();
    Thread thread1 = new Thread(new ThreadStart(jollythread.OurThread));
    Thread thread2 = new Thread(new ThreadStart(jollythread.OurThread));
    thread1.Name="Graham"; thread2.Name="Desdemona";
    // Both of these threads are synchronized / locked:
    // thread1 will be processed until completion before thread2 begins
    thread1.Start();
    thread2.Start();
    }
```

The output of Listing 7-11 is as follows:

```
(This thread is Running with Normal priority)
Graham has been working for 0 hours
Graham has been working for 1 hours
Graham has been working for 2 hours
```

```
(This thread is Running with Normal priority)
Desdemona has been working for 0 hours
Desdemona has been working for 1 hours
Desdemona has been working for 2 hours
```

Without the locking mechanism in place, we would see lines about Graham and Desdemona alternating in this work-related status update. You'll also see three properties of the Threading class being displayed in their full glory (i.e., *ThreadState*, *Priority*, and *Name*).

## Sleep vs. Yield

So far we've explored the use of the Sleep method in several of our listings. To reiterate, this tells a thread to take a nap/suspend itself for a predetermined duration usually specified in milliseconds.

It's time we bring in the C# *Yield*. This keyword has multiple meanings in C# depending on the context; we'll examine them in more detail in the next chapter. In a multithreaded environment, Yield tells a thread to enter a state of indeterminate waiting. A yielded thread will be reactivated whenever needed; this may occur within just a few milliseconds or take a much longer time. Yield basically frees the CPU from executing a specific thread in order to process other, more urgent threads. The level of this urgency is ultimately decided on by one's operating system.

---

The C# Yield can actually be emulated to some degree by the Sleep method. Older .NET frameworks (prior to version 4.0) were not yet Yield capable. In those cases, typing in Sleep(0) worked similar to Yield.

---

Let's now take a gander at how Yield performs in action (see Listing 7-12).

**Listing 7-12.** *A listing demonstrating the Yield method in C#*

```
using System;
using System.Threading;
public class AmazingThreads
{
private int counter; // Declare a counter-variable
    public void YieldThread()
    {
        Console.WriteLine("First thread is an infinite loop with Yield()");
        while(true) // Start an infinite loop
        {
```

```
        // Without Yield, the counter would trail off to much longer lengths
        Thread.Yield();
        ++counter;
        }
    }
    public void SecondThread()
    {
Console.WriteLine("Second thread informs you: First thread counter reached "
+ counter);
    }
}
public class YieldExample
{
    public static void Main()
    {
        AmazingThreads greatobject = new AmazingThreads();
        Thread thread1 = new Thread(new ThreadStart(greatobject.YieldThread));
        Thread thread2 = new Thread(new ThreadStart(greatobject.SecondThread));
        thread1.Start();
        thread2.Start();
    }
}
```

In Listing 7-12, we define a class integer, *counter*, to roughly document the length of the first thread's execution time prior to Yield kicking in. We then start two threads, the first of them entering an infinite loop. The second thread is there to display the amount stored in the counter-variable. With Yield, we can expect this to read well under 2000 under most scenarios. Without Yield, the counter will display a reading several orders of magnitude higher, eventually causing the program to become unresponsive.

Again, the operating system is the ultimate entity scheduling the thread making a Yield request, according to the status and priorities of other threads.

# Join

One of the most important methods for threaded work in C# is called *Join*. With this method, you make threads wait while others are done processing. Naturally, Join can only be called by a thread that has already started its execution (see Listing 7-13).

**Listing 7-13.** *A basic demonstration of the Join method in C#*

```
using System;
using System.Threading;
static void OurFunction() { // Create a custom method
            for (int i = 0; i < 10; ++i)
            Console.Write(i + " ");
        }

static void Main(string[] args) {
            Thread thread1 = new Thread(OurFunction);
            thread1.Start();
            thread1.Join();
            // Join() makes sure a thread completes its processing
            // before the listing proceeds
            Console.Write("10"); // Finish the list with a number ten
}
```

Listing 7-13 provides us with a rudimentary example of the Join method. The output from Listing 7-13 should be *0 1 2 3 4 5 6 7 8 9 10*. Without Join, you might get unexpected results, such as *100 1 2 3 4 5 6 7 8 9*. This is because the last *Console.Write* is not specifically told to wait until *thread1* completes its processing.

# Going Asynchronous in C#

Basically, *asynchronous programming* is the art of having a program consist of numerous tasks which are not going to get in conflict with each other (or other programs). This approach is also often easier on the programmer's eyes as it results in a rather clear layout of code.

The current implementation of asynchronous processing in C# leverages a class called *ThreadPool*. This class takes a different approach to the Thread-class (discussed earlier in this chapter). For one, ThreadPool only creates background threads with low priorities; assigning priorities to threads isn't a part of this class.

---

A *design pattern* is a reusable solution to a repeatedly occurring problem inside a specific context in software design.

---

Now, there are three major asynchronous programming paradigms in C#. Only one of them, TAP, is recommended for use by Microsoft as of 2021.

- **Asynchronous programming model (APM)**: The APM approach uses the *IAsyncResult* interface and its *BeginOperationName* and *EndOperationName* methods. Microsoft no longer recommends using this somewhat arduous design pattern.

- **Event-based asynchronous pattern (EAP)**: EAP was devised to offer the benefits of the asynchronous software paradigm while keeping things relatively graceful from the programmer's perspective. This design pattern, too, is considered an outdated approach.

- **Task-based asynchronous pattern (TAP)**: TAP is the most up-to-date and elegant design pattern for writing asynchronous software. Unlike APM and EAP, TAP uses a single method to represent the initiation and completion of an asynchronous operation and is centered around the *Task* and *Task<TResult>* classes.

For an example of an asynchronous pattern using TAP, see Listing 7-14.

**Listing 7-14.** *A demonstration of asynchronous processing in C# using the TAP design pattern*

```
using System;
using System.Threading;
static async Task Main(string[] args) // Our small asynchronous main thread
    {
        await happyMethod(); // Await for happyMethod to do its thing
            Console.WriteLine("Program complete.");
    }

public static async Task happyMethod() // Create asynchronous Task happyMethod()
    {
        int fibo = await Fibonacci(); // Await  for  Fibonacci-method  to
                                    complete
            // and assign its results into integer "fibo"
        DisplayFibonacci(fibo); // Summon our most simple method
    }
public static async Task<int> Fibonacci()
// Create asynchronous Task Fibonacci(), which is to return an integer
    {
            int x = 0, y = 1, z = 0; // Define  variables  needed  in  our
                                    for-loop
            // This task is kept simple for the sake of clarity. In real life
            // you could do some heavy lifting here in concert with other
            // asynchronous tasks.
```

```
            await Task.Run(() =>
            {
                for (int i = 2; i < 5; i++) // Look for Fibonacci number
                {
    z = x + y;
    x = y;
    y = z;
                }
        });
        return z; // Return result, i.e. the fifth Fibonacci
    }

public static void DisplayFibonacci(int fibo) // Method for display the result
    {
        Console.WriteLine("The fifth Fibonacci number is " + fibo);
    }
```

Now, Listing 7-14 is split into four methods of which only one isn't asynchronous in nature (i.e., *DisplayFibonacci*). The first three methods use the *async/await* mechanism. By using the definition *async* next to a method, we designate a method to be asynchronous. This allows us to then use the await keyword, which yields control to its calling method.

The async/await mechanism allows programs to work on potentially heavy calculations in the background, which often results in less glitchy user interfaces and/or faster network file transfers.

When creating methods, TAP has some specific keywords. *Task* is there to denote methods which don't return any values. In our listing, you'll also find one instance of a *Task<int>*; this expression denotes a method which must return an integer. Tasks may return any type of variable. All asynchronous tasks created will be scheduled to run on threads managed by the ThreadPool class.

The command *await Task.Run* starts a task in its very own thread using the class ThreadPool. Now, there are basically three ways to invoke this mechanic:

```
1       await Task.Run(() => SomeMethod );
2       await Task.Run(() => SomeOtherMethod(something) );
3       await Task.Run(() => {
        Console.WriteLine("Let's do something here");
        return 0;
        });
```

The first approach accepts previously declared methods without parameters; you simply pass the name of a method. The second approach is for methods which take arguments. We can also use *block-based* syntax, as demonstrated by the third mechanic. As always, care must be taken with the correct use of parentheses, curly brackets, and other special characters. As you probably noticed, Listing 7-7 used the block-based approach for its *await Task.Run( )*.

---

In a *Fibonacci sequence*, each number represents the sum of two numbers preceding it, for example, 0, 1, 1, 2, 3, 5, 8. The concept was introduced by Italian mathematician *Leonardo Bonacci (b. 1170, d. possibly 1250)* in his seminal work *Liber Abaci*. At some point in his life, Bonacci was given Fibonacci as a nickname.

---

# In Closing

Finishing this chapter, you'll have probably learned quite a bit on the following:

- Some popular uses for the C# System.Globalization namespace and some of its classes, including Calendar and CultureInfo

- Basic file operations in C# using File and FileInfo classes

- The basics of garbage collection (GC) in C#

- The implementation of basic multithreading in C#, including some of the most relevant associated methods (Join, Start, Sleep, Yield)

- The basics of asynchronous programming in C# using the task-based asynchronous design pattern (TAP) and its async/await mechanism

Chapter 8 is dedicated to the even finer techniques provided by C#, Java, and Python, including advanced multithreading. We'll be entering the world of making useful (but decidedly small-scale) applications.

# Graduation Day: Slightly Larger Programming Projects

In this chapter, we examine several slightly larger programming projects in Python, C#, and Java than so far presented. These projects are designed to demonstrate some of the most relevant concepts discussed in this book: variables, loops, file access, and threading. If you are able to decipher these little projects' innards, you can safely say you have a level of understanding on the basics of the three programming languages featured in this book. And if you still feel unsure about your skills as a coder at this point, this chapter can help you clarify some concepts.

© Robert Ciesla 2021
R. Ciesla, *Programming Basics*, https://doi.org/10.1007/978-1-4842-7286-2_8

# The Universal Chatting Simulator for Python

We'll start this chapter by introducing the *Universal Chatting Simulator* to the world. This program will demonstrate the following features of Python, all of which we have discussed previously in the book:

- File operations
- String formatting
- Custom function definition (using the def keyword)
- Variables (including randomizing), lists, and iteration
- Basic exception handling
- Element enumeration
- Program flow and simple loops
- Date and time retrieval

Like the other programs in this chapter, the Universal Chatting Simulator (UCS) is a console application, meaning it works in text mode only; no graphical elements will be used to keep it simple.

Now, the two key elements of UCS come in the form of a virtual chat host and their virtual audience, the latter being portrayed by a shared moniker of "chat." Both of these virtual actors output text onscreen every few seconds, the contents of which are determined by three external, and thus easily editable, text files.

---

There's no need to type the entire listing to begin experimenting with the UCS; the file is available on GitHub where this freely downloadable listing is also fully commented. However, let's now go through the program block by block just to be thorough.

---

# Part One: Setting Up the Project

First, we import the required code modules. *Datetime*, *time*, and *random* come with Python. However, for our project, we also need to acquire an additional module from the *Python Package Index (PyPI)*. This is a free online repository for extending Python's functionality. We'll be using the asset *clrprint* by Abhijith Boppe. After installing and importing the clrprint module, we can add colorful text into our Python projects with lines like this: *clrprint("Hello!", clr='red')*. See Listing 8-1 for the first part of the project code.

Install *clrprint* simply by entering *"pip3 install clrprint"* into the macOS terminal, Windows shell, or Linux command line.

*Listing 8-1.* First part of the listing for the Universal Chatting Simulator in Python

```python
# import three Python code-modules
import datetime
import time
import random
# also import the clrprint-module from the Python Package Index (PyPI)
from clrprint import *
name = "Apple representative"  # virtual chat host name
mood = 50   # moods: 50 = neutral, 0 = bad ending, 100 = good ending
score = messages_sent = 0  # assign zero to score and messages_sent
response = negative = positive = False  # assign False to three variables
negativetrigger = "orange"  # negative trigger word, used to reduce mood
positivetrigger = "apple"  # positive trigger word, used to grow mood
# Fetch current time and date using now() from datetime-class
initial_time = datetime.datetime.now()
# define a custom function, print_chat()
# variable "cap" decides how the chat messages are to be capitalized, if at all
# both 0 and -1 mean no changes in capitalization
# 1 means capitalize first letter of a line, 2 means capitalize all letters
in a line
def print_chat(chat):
                cap = random.choice([-1, 0, 1, 2])
                if cap == 1:
                chat = chat.capitalize()  # summon capitalize() method
                elif cap == 2:
                chat = chat.upper()  # summon upper() method for ALL CAPS
                print("Chat: " + timer.strftime("<%A %H:%M> ") + chat)
```

Next, we define a custom function called *open_chatfile* which takes two arguments, *name* and *deletechar*. Name simply represents the file name we want to open. Deletechar is used to denote a character we are to delete from these lists; this is there, so we may, for one, delete all newline characters (i.e., \n) from the chat to eliminate unnecessary blank lines (see Listing 8-2).

We also use a temporary list structure, *templist,* in our function. Data is fed into templist so that it may be enumerated and have its newline characters removed. The file contents are read using Python's readlines method.

*Listing 8-2.* *The second part of the listing for the Universal Chatting Simulator in Python*

```python
def open_chatfile(name, deletechar):
    try:
        file = open(name, 'r')  # open file in read-only mode, "r"
        print("Loading file " + name)

        templist = file.readlines()  # read file into templist
        for i, element in enumerate(templist):  # enumerate the list
            templist[i] = element.replace(deletechar, '') # delete newlines
        return templist  # return the enumerated list
        file.close()  # closing the file is always a good practice
    except (FileNotFoundError, IOError):  # handle an exception
        # str() converts variables to string
        print("The file " + str(name) + " could not be read!")
```

# Part Two: Displaying Highscores

Before we get to score keeping, we are to define three lists for use with our open_chatfile function; they are called *neutralmoods*, *badmoods*, and *chatmoods*. The data from text files needs to be stored somewhere, and this is where our three lists come in (see Listing 8-3).

---

In Python, we can initialize variables, including lists, with the same variable and on the same line using the assignment operator, for example, *a = b = 10* or *happy = wonderful = [ ]*.

---

Next, we actually use our method, summoning it thrice to open the files *neutral.txt*, *bad.txt*, and *chat.txt*. The other two arguments open_chatfile takes are the lists we previously created and the newline characters. Now, we have three lists full of thought-provoking communication ready for our virtual chatting pleasure.

Ending this block of the project, we are to open a text file containing the currently reigning high score. Yes, we have a scoring system in the Universal Chatting Simulator; more on this later. We go about fetching our score data by creating a try block. As a reminder, a try block allows us to test our code for errors on the fly. Coupled with the except keyword (short for exception), we can introduce our very own error messages. Inside the try block in Listing 8-3 an attempt is made to load the file *highscores.txt*. If such a file can't be found, the exception block is there to tell us so and create the file.

**Listing 8-3.** *The third part of the listing for the Universal Chatting Simulator in Python*

```python
# display program title in vibrant yellow using the clrprint-module
clrprint("Universal Chatting Simulator (UCS) ver 0.1.0 by Bob the Developer",
clr='yellow')

# define three list-structures to be filled with data from text-files
neutralmoods = badmoods = chatmoods = []  # [] denotes an empty list
# insert textfile-data into the three lists using our custom function
neutralmoods = open_chatfile("neutral.txt", "\n")
badmoods = open_chatfile("bad.txt", "\n")
chatmoods = open_chatfile("chat.txt", "\n")
print("Your starting mood is " + str(mood) + "/100")

# display current highscore stored in "highscore.txt"
try:
    # open "highscore.txt" in r+ mode for both reading and writing
    with open("highscore.txt", "r+") as scorefile:
        hiscore = scorefile.read()
        print("CURRENT HIGHSCORE: %s" % hiscore)
# if highscore.txt is not found, create this file
except (FileNotFoundError, IOError):
    print("Highscores not found. Creating highscore.txt")

    scorefile = open("highscore.txt", "w")
    scorefile.write("0")  # write zero into "highscore.txt"
    scorefile.close()
```

# Part Three: The Indomitable Main Loop

Now, we enter the realm of the main loop. This is where most of the processing and/or magic happens. UCS runs in a while loop, which reads "while variable mood is smaller than 100." If mood reaches over a hundred, the loop is no longer run. In addition, the loop is exited using a break keyword if mood falls under one.

The virtual chatters get their representation in the proceedings using the variable simply called *chat*; an element is selected at random from the chatmoods list and input into this variable to be displayed further down in Listing 8-4.

You may wonder what the hubbub was about variable *mood*. Not only is mood used to break out of the main loop, but if it reaches under 30, the program will start using a different set of lines for our virtual host (i.e., the more sour ones as defined in the file *bad.txt*). The value of the mood integer is affected by specific keywords, namely, two more variables *negativetrigger* and *positivetrigger*, defined earlier in Listing 8-1. If the program detects a negative trigger word, "mood" is reduced by a number between 1 and 5. Similarly, a positive trigger word results in the integer being added to by a number between 1 and 5. For this purpose, we use the line *random.randint(1, 5)* to generate an integer number inside the desired range, assigning it to yet another variable, *moodchange*.

Now, two boolean variables are there to raise a flag if a trigger word is detected in Listing 8-4; these are simply called *negative* and *positive*. These two booleans are used to display status messages about any mood changes later in the program.

# Capitalization and Delays

Next, we add a little cosmetic variety into the proceedings. Listing 8-4 can present all of the chat lines in three types of formatting: regular, first letter capitalized, and all caps. This is achieved by examining the randomized value of variable *cap* once every main loop. We issue cap four potential values: -1, 0, 1, and 2. Should cap stay below 1, a line of chatter remains untouched. A value of 1 makes the program summon Python's *capitalize()* method, which does what its name implies. Finally, a value of 2 corresponds with the *upper()* method, basically turning on the caps lock for our virtual chatters (for one line only).

For a program simulating a chat, some delays must be implemented so that the viewer may fully enjoy the flow of the moderately insightful commentary. In Listing 8-4, we do this by applying Python's wonderful sleep() method and feeding it a random value between 1 and 3, corresponding with an equal number of seconds of delay.

**Listing 8-4.** *The fourth part of the listing for the Universal Chatting Simulator in Python*

```python
# main while-loop begins
while 1 < mood < 100:  # keep looping as long as mood remains under 100
    timer = datetime.datetime.now()  # Fetch current time and date

    chat = random.choice(chatmoods) # Select a random line from "chatmoods"

    if negativetrigger in chat:  # negative trigger word found
            # set variable "moodchange" between one and five
        moodchange = random.randint(1, 5)
        mood -= moodchange
            negative = True  # negative trigger word was found
    if positivetrigger in chat:  # positive trigger word found
        moodchange = random.randint(1, 5)
        mood += moodchange
        positive = True  # positive trigger word was found
            print_chat(chat) # summon function for printing chat's output
```

```
messages_sent = messages_sent + 1
if negative:   # same as "if negative == True:"
    if mood < 0:
        mood = 0
    clrprint("MOOD -" + str(moodchange) + "! Your current mood is
    " + str(mood) + "/100", clr='red')
    negative = False
if positive:   # same as "if positive == True:"
    clrprint("MOOD +" + str(moodchange) + "! Your current mood is
    " + str(mood) + "/100", clr='green')
    positive = False
# delay program between one to three seconds
time.sleep(random.randint(1, 3))
# set a 50% of chance for a response from our virtual chat host
response = random.choice([True, False])
if response:
    if mood > 30:
        clrprint(
            name + ": " + timer.strftime("<%A %H:%M> ") +
            random.choice(neutralmoods),
            clr='white')
    else:
        clrprint(name + ": " + timer.strftime("<%A %H:%M> ") +
        random.choice(badmoods),
                clr='white')
```

# Part Four: Game Over

After a pretty busy main loop, we finally reach the last segment in our chatting simulator. It mainly consists of taking care of score keeping with a bit of path branching added for good measure (see Listing 8-5).

The scoring in the program is based on the amount of chat messages sent by the virtual chatters; each message is worth three points. Now, there are two endings to this simulator program. In the "bad" one, the viewer is simply told the virtual chat host's mood fell to zero. The other, more upbeat ending grants the viewer a "euphoria bonus" worth 1000 points.

*Listing 8-5. The fifth and final part of the listing for the Universal Chatting Simulator in Python*

```
# game over
score = messages_sent * 3   # make each message from chat worth 3 points

if mood < 1:   # bad ending
    clrprint("Your mood fell to 0/100!", clr='yellow')
```

```python
else:  # good ending
    clrprint("Your mood reached 100/100!", clr='yellow')
    clrprint("Euphoria bonus: 1000", clr='yellow')
    score = score + 1000  # add euphoria bonus to score

timespent = timer - initial_time  # calculate elapsed time
print("Time spent in the chat: " + str(timespent))
print("Your chat sent " + str(messages_sent) + " messages")
print("SCORE: " + str(score))
# if current score is greater than saved highscore, save that to file
with open("highscore.txt", "r+") as scorefile:
    hiscore = scorefile.read()
    if not hiscore:  # if file is empty..
        hiscore = '0'  # ..assign zero into it
    if score > int(hiscore):  # if current score is greater than the
    stored highscore
        print("NEW HIGHSCORE MADE!")
        scorefile.seek(0)  # "rewind" to the beginning of the file
        scorefile.write(score)  # write the new score into "highscore.txt"
    else:
        print("CURRENT HIGHSCORE: %s" % hiscore)
```

We have quite a few methods at work in Listing 8-4. As a recap, let's document the main Python methods used by the Universal Chatting Simulator (see Table 8-1).

**Table 8-1.** Some Python methods used by the Universal Chatting Simulator

| Method | Description | Example of use in Listing 8-4 |
|---|---|---|
| open() | Open file for reading and/or writing | file = open(name, 'r') |
| read() | Read contents of an open file | hiscore = scorefile.read() |
| seek() | Set a file's position | scorefile.seek(0) |
| random. randint() | Return a random integer | neutralmoods[random.randint(0, len(neutralmoods) - 1)], |
| random. choice() | Choose an element at random | response = random.choice([True, False]) |
| str() | Convert variable to string | print("SCORE: " + str(score)) |
| int() | Return an integer object | if score > int(hiscore): |
| len() | Return object/string length | |

# Thread Racer for C#

To refresh your memory on how threading works in C#, take a peek at Listing 8-6. In this little listing, three threads are sent to run a five-meter dash. The program demonstrates the following features of the C# language:

- Simple threading and thread-based access to shared data/variables

- Using locking objects and the Interlocked.Decrement() method

- Assigning random values to variables, including string arrays

- Defining methods (e.g., MakeNames) and retrieving data from them

**Listing 8-6.** *A program demonstrating threading in C#*

```
using System;
using System.Threading;
public class ThreadRacer
{
// Define an empty (i.e. null) string for holding the winner of the race
string winner = null;
// Define an integer for examining the threads' arrival order at finishing line
int place = 3;
// Create an object, happylock, for thread-locking purposes
static object happylock = new object();
        // Define Racer, a thread-based method
        public void Racer()
        {
                int distance = 5; // Set racing distance to 5

                // Assign variable "handle" with the current thread so we may read
                // thread properties, such as Name
                Thread handle = Thread.CurrentThread;
        // Loop while a thread's distance is greater than zero
while(distance > 0) {
Console.WriteLine(handle.Name+" is at " + distance + " meters from the goal.");
// Reduce racer's distance by one using an Interlocked.Decrement-method
Interlocked.Decrement(ref distance);
                }
// Summon our locking object
lock(happylock) {
// If the winner-variable is still set to "null", announce current thread
// as the winner
        if(winner == null) Console.WriteLine(handle.Name + " WON 1st place!");
```

```
// Use an Interlocked.Decrement-method to subtract 1 from variable "place"
        Interlocked.Decrement(ref place);
winner = handle.Name;
            if(place==1) Console.WriteLine(handle.Name + " came in 2ND..");
            if(place==0) Console.WriteLine(handle.Name + " came in 3RD..");
            }
    }
    public static string MakeNames() {
    // create new object, random0, using the C# Random class
    var random0 = new Random();
    // Create two string-arrays, first_names and last_names
    string[] first_names = { "Peter", "Paul", "Patrick", "Patricia",
    "Priscilla", "Pauline" };
    string[] last_names = { "Plonker", "Pillock", "Prat", "Pecker" };
    int f_index = random0.Next(first_names.Length);
    int l_index = random0.Next(last_names.Length);
    // return name as a string:
    return (first_names[f_index] + " " + last_names[l_index]);
    }
    public static void Main() // Main function
     {
     ThreadRacer racer = new ThreadRacer();
     Thread thread1 = new Thread(new ThreadStart(racer.Racer));
     Thread thread2 = new Thread(new ThreadStart(racer.Racer));
    Thread thread3 = new Thread(new ThreadStart(racer.Racer));
            thread1.Name = "[Racer A] " + MakeNames();
            thread2.Name = "[Racer B] " + MakeNames();
            thread3.Name = "[Racer C] " + MakeNames();
            Console.WriteLine("Welcome to THREAD RACER!\n");
            thread1.Start(); // Start threads
            thread2.Start();
            thread3.Start();
            }
    }
}
```

In Listing 8-6, we made a locking object, happylock, for thread synchronization. We also used a new method, Interlocked.Decrement, to decrease the "distance" and "place" variables by exactly one. For effective and safe addition in a thread-based project, C# also provides a method known as Interlocked. Increment (which we didn't need for Thread Racer). These two methods can often replace the standard subtraction and addition operators (e.g., --variable or ++variable) when working with thread-based code in C#.

Now, we crafted one method of our own in Listing 8-6; this would be *MakeNames*. This method is there to demonstrate arrays, more specifically those of the string variety. These arrays are populated with names and returned as a single string for use by the main function.

The *f_index* and *l_index* variables in Thread Racer are there to store the desired index positions of the string arrays *first_names* and *last_names*. These index positions are in turn created by applying a Next method, a randomizer, on the arrays' lengths. These lengths are then deduced by summoning the aptly named Length method.

Here's one of those lines of codes in Listing 8-6:

```
int f_index = random0.Next(first_names.Length);
```

This reads: "have integer *f_index* equal a **random number** with a maximum value of the **length** of the *first_names*-array." Rolls right off the tongue.

We can add output from methods straight into variables. Take this line from Listing 8-6, for example: *thread1.Name = "[Racer A] " + MakeNames();* in which we combine the string "[Racer A"] with whatever MakeNames happens to output, using but a simple plus operator.

---

The thread scheduling for Thread Racer, too, is performed by the operating system. This means you may get the same results after a while.

---

# Jolly Quiz for C#

Next up, Listing 8-7 presents to you a little console-based quiz program. It demonstrates the following features of this fine language:

- Basic file operations and threading
- String formatting
- Program flow, user interaction, and loops
- Variables and iteration

Jolly Quiz uses two separate files, *questions.txt* and *answers.txt*. Both of them are processed from the top down with each line in the question file corresponding with the same line in the answers file. This approach makes it easy to add new questions and modify existing ones simply by editing the two text files.

The user is expected to type their answer during program execution. A threaded object runs in the background, independent of the quiz in progress, telling the user to "hurry up!" every four seconds. Every correct answer grants ten points. At the end of the quiz, the user is presented with their score as well as the percentage of correct answers.

*Listing 8-7.* *A quiz program in C# demonstrating basic file operations and threading*

```csharp
using System;
using System.IO;
using System.Threading;
class JollyQuiz
{
    public static void Main()
    {
    // Declare three integer-variables
    int counter=0, score=0, percentage=0;
    // Declare a boolean-variable (takes: true or false)
    bool countdown=true;
    Console.WriteLine("Welcome to THE JOLLY QUIZ PROGRAM!\n");
    // Create a new thread-object, timerthread1
      Thread timerthread1 = new Thread(delegate() {
      Thread.Sleep(6000); // Sleep for 6 seconds at first
    while(true) { // Create an infinite loop inside our thread
          Console.WriteLine("HURRY UP!");
          Thread.Sleep(4000);
      // End thread processing if countdown is set to "false" in main program
      if(!countdown) break; // This reads: if countdown is NOT "true" exit
      loop
    }
      });
    // Open the question and answer -files. These should work from the
    // same directory as your project file
    var q = File.ReadAllLines("questions.txt");
    var a = File.ReadAllLines("answers.txt");
    timerthread1.Start(); // Start the timer-thread

    foreach(string lines in q) // Iterate through the questions-file
        {
        Console.WriteLine("{0}\nEnter response: ", lines);
    // Convert response to ALL CAPS to eliminate input capitalization issues
    // i.e. make "Helsinki" equally valid to "HeLSiNKI"
    string response = Console.ReadLine().ToUpper();
        ++counter;
        // Compare user input against correct answers
        if(response.Equals(a[counter-1])) {
        Console.WriteLine("{0} is correct!", response); score+=10;
    // use else if to determine whether the user wrote a wrong answer
    // or simply pressed enter
    } else if(response!="") Console.WriteLine("{0} is wrong..", response);
            else Console.WriteLine("Type something next time!");
        }
    // No need to remind the user to hurry up after the quiz is over;
    // so we next tell timerthread1 to end processing
```

```
       countdown = false;
       Console.Write("\nYour score: {0}. ", score);
       percentage = score*100/(counter*10);
       Console.WriteLine("You knew/guessed {0}% right on the {1} questions
       presented.", percentage, counter);
       // Display shaming message for motivation after a poor score
       if(percentage < 50) Console.WriteLine("Shame on you!");
       // Display a different message for a more impressive score
       if(percentage >= 90) Console.WriteLine("Well done!");
       }
  }
```

You'll notice Listings 8-6 and 8-7 feature a peculiar variable type, *var*. This is an *implicit variable definition* in C# and simply means the compiler program is allowed to determine the type of a variable. For smaller projects in C#, this approach usually works just fine.

# A Recipe Book in Java

We'll next return to the world of Java with a little program called *Delicious Finnish Recipes*. This rather straightforward listing basically displays easily customized text files.

*Listing 8-8.* *A program in Java demonstrating file access*

```java
import java.io.File;
import java.io.FileNotFoundException;
import java.util.Scanner;

public class FinnishRecipes {
  // Define LoadText, a method for loading text-files
  // which takes a file path and filename as its arguments
  static void LoadText(String path1, String section) {
    try {
    File fileobject1 = new File(path1 + section);
    // Create a Scanner-object, reader1, for user input
    Scanner reader1 = new Scanner(fileobject1);
    while (reader1.hasNextLine()) {
      String output1 = reader1.nextLine();
      System.out.println(output1);
    }
     reader1.close();
  } catch (FileNotFoundException e) { // Throw exception/error if needed
    System.out.println("File " + section + " not found!");
  }
 }
```

```java
static void DisplayMenu() {
System.out.println("DELICIOUS FINNISH RECIPES\nEnter choice:");
System.out.println("[1] Salads");
System.out.println("[2] Main Courses");
System.out.println("[3] Custom recipes (make your own)");
System.out.println("[4] Quit)");
}
// Define Main method
public static void main(String[] args) {
    // Display main menu
    DisplayMenu();
    Scanner keyscanner1 = new Scanner(System.in);

    while(true) { // Create an infinite while-loop
    String input1 = keyscanner1.nextLine();
    // "C:\\" refers to the file-path to the most common Windows root-drive
    // modify this path as per your file locations
    if(input1.equals("1")) LoadText("","salads.txt");
    if(input1.equals("2")) LoadText("","maincourses.txt");
    if(input1.equals("3")) LoadText("","custom.txt");
    if(input1.equals("4")) break;

    // Display menu again if user inputs a plain enter
    if(input1.equals("")) DisplayMenu();
    } System.out.println("Have a great day!");
  }
}
```

In Listing 8-8, we create a method, *LoadText,* which takes two arguments, namely, the file path and name. It then proceeds to load the specified text file and display its contents, line by line, on screen. We also have another method, *DisplayMenu,* which is simply used to display the options available to the user. Both methods are defined as *void,* which means they are to return no information.

There is a try-catch block in Listing 8-8 which will sound off, that is, throw an exception, if a file is not found. An infinite while loop keeps the program running until the user enters "4" on their keyboard, in which case a break keyword is executed.

# A Stopwatch in Java

The following program acts as a simple stopwatch. You input a number of seconds for it to crunch, before it lets you know you're out of time. This program represents a very basic implementation of threading in Java, consisting of a single main thread.

**Listing 8-9.** *A listing for a stopwatch program in Java*

```java
import java.util.Scanner;
public class Counter {
  public static void main(String[] args) {
  int counter1=0;
  Scanner keyscanner1 = new Scanner(System.in);

  // Loop while counter1 equals zero
  while(counter1 <= 0) {
  System.out.println("Enter timer count (in seconds): ");
  String input1 = keyscanner1.nextLine();
  // begin a try-catch block
  try {
  // Convert "input1" to integer
  counter1 = Integer.parseInt(input1);
  } catch (NumberFormatException e) {
    System.out.println("Enter value in numbers only!");
  }
  if(counter1<0) System.out.println("(Positive numbers only!)");
  } // Loop end

  // Loop while counter is greater than zero
  while(counter1 > 0) {
  System.out.println("Time left: " + counter1 + " sec");
  try
  { Thread.sleep(1000); }
  catch(InterruptedException ex)
  { Thread.currentThread().interrupt(); }
  --counter1;
  } // Second loop end
  System.out.println("All done!");
  }
}
```

Listing 8-9 has two while loops. The first one is there to take input from the user and make sure this conforms to specific rules. Mainly, the input is to consist of positive numbers only. The program throws an exception, a *NumberFormatException* to be precise, should letters or other non-numeric characters be entered. Additionally, the first loop refuses to accept negative numbers and posts a message about it if need be.

In the second loop, we use a line with *Thread.sleep(1000)* to experience the desired amount of delay. Do note that for the sleep method to work in Java, you need to check it for exceptions. In Listing 8-9, we used a classic try-catch block for this purpose.

## In Closing

Finishing this chapter, you'll have refreshed your memory on the following aspects of Python, C#, and Java:

- Data structures, program flow, and basic file operations
- Elementary threading techniques
- Exception handling using the try-catch block
- Function definition and access

Chapter 9 will be much lighter on the code, being all about some lovely diagrams, namely, those created with the *Universal Modeling Language (UML)*.

# UML Class Diagrams

This chapter is dedicated to the wonders of the Unified Modeling Language, which is a rather ubiquitous tool in software design—and deservedly so. Having only touched the surface of UML previously in this book, we'll now go in deeper and explore more of the possibilities UML offers as it pertains to class modeling.

## Visualizing the Object-Oriented Paradigm

We introduced the object-oriented paradigm in Chapter 4. Most of the code listings in the book are indeed of this paradigm in nature with their classes, objects, and methods. Think of UML as a valuable tool in the pre-coding phase of software development. You plot out all of the OOP-related mechanisms with it, including classes and their relations with other classes.

The Universal Modeling Language comes in two standards, namely, UML 1.x (originally from 1996) and UML 2.x (first released in 2005). Both of these standards consist of numerous types of diagrams for practically any modeling purpose.

© Robert Ciesla 2021
R. Ciesla, *Programming Basics*, https://doi.org/10.1007/978-1-4842-7286-2_9

# The Categories of UML Diagrams

The entire spectrum of UML diagram types is out of the scope of this book. However, it's useful to know what varieties UML comes in. Broadly speaking, it's usually divided into two main categories which are then divided into numerous subcategories. Many larger projects might need most of the following (non-exhaustive) list of diagrams; they are mutually exclusive with each other.

- **Structural diagrams**: These types of diagrams are there to model the nature of a system at rest.
    1. **Class diagrams**: These are perhaps the most commonly used diagrams in UML. We will mainly focus on class diagrams in this chapter. As you may have guessed, they deal with the class aspect which is the basis for the object-oriented programming (OOP) paradigm.
    2. **Object diagrams**: Obviously related to class diagrams, object diagrams describe the instances of classes. These types of diagrams are often used when building a prototype for a system.
    3. **Component diagrams**: These diagrams focus on the types of software components within a system as well as their connections. These components are often referred to as physical assets, although technically they tend to reside purely on a digital level.
    4. **Deployment diagrams**: These are used for visualizing a system's complete layout, with both the physical and software parts of a system on display. A deployment diagram can also be called a topology of system components.
- **Behavioral diagrams**: Unlike those of the structural variety, behavioral diagrams are centered on mapping out a system in action.
    1. **Use cases**: An actor in UML is a party who interacts with a system. Use case diagrams depict the interactions between (human) actors and specific systems. Use cases focus on particular functionalities a system provides. For example, a person withdrawing money from an ATM is one potential scenario for a use case diagram.

2. **Sequence diagrams**: These diagrams focus on the time sequence of messages sent by objects. So when the interactions between objects are to be accurately modeled, we use a UML sequence diagram.

3. **State-chart diagrams**: States in UML mean the different varieties of information an object holds, but not their behavior. State-chart diagrams are used when modeling changes to the state of a system.

4. **Activity diagrams**: When we need to visualize the control flow within a system, this is the type of diagram to use. Basically, an activity diagram provides an idea of how a system will work upon execution.

# Getting Back to UML: Class Diagrams

As previously discussed, UML can be used to model pretty much anything, and a *class diagram* is there to help us visualize an object-oriented software project. Let's start with something simple (see Figure 9-1).

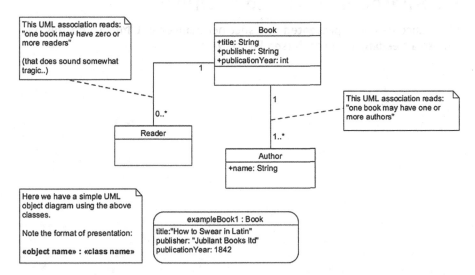

**Figure 9-1.** A simple UML class/object diagram

Figure 9-1 demonstrates classes, including their variables and methods and interclass relationships in UML; it also features a single UML object diagram.

The main class in Figure 9-1 is called Book. It has three variables (i.e., title, publisher, and publication year). As you can see, we need to specify the type of variable in the classes as well (e.g., String). A plus (+) in front of an attribute or method in UML denotes a public access modifier. Class members with a dash (-) character signify a private access modifier.

---

You can add helpful notes straight into UML diagrams as we did in Figure 9-1; these are to take the form of rectangles with folded upper right corners.

---

Now, simple lines mark the associations between classes and other entities in UML. The numbers and asterisks next to these lines in Figure 9-1 are a demonstration of *multiplicity* in UML. This concept is used to indicate how many instances (i.e., objects) a class can provide or be allowed to interact with.

Moving on to the object part of Figure 9-1, we have a single instance of the main class, called *exampleBook1*. Objects can be represented as boxes of either sharp or round edges in UML; we opted for the latter for variety.

## Tree-Based Inheritance in UML

Inheritance can be represented in a succinct manner in UML. To do this, we can use a *tree-based* approach (see Figure 9-2).

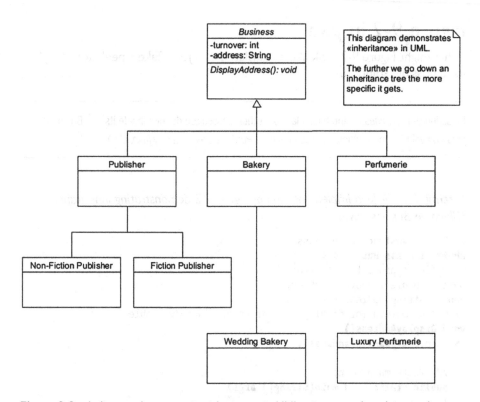

**Figure 9-2.** A diagram demonstrating inheritance in UML using a tree-based approach

The diagram in Figure 9-2 demonstrates three levels of specialization. First, you have the generic Business class. This is followed by three specialized classes, namely, Publisher, Bakery, and Perfumerie. Finally, we have the most specialized level of two different types of publisher classes, a class for Wedding Bakery and Luxury Perfumerie for good measure.

---

In OOP, parlance base classes are also known as *parent classes*. Subclasses are often called *child classes.*

---

The Business class in Figure 9-2 is defined as *abstract*; in UML, a class name in italics denotes this. These classes are there to provide specific methods for the subclasses to inherit. Abstract classes cannot be directly instantiated. Instead, you create objects using one of their non-abstract (i.e., concrete) subclasses.

# Figure 9-2 in Java

What might Figure 9-2 look like if translated into Java? Take a peek at Listing 9-1 for a possible solution.

---

In Listing 9-1, *Business* is the base class. All other classes are defined inside its file, Business. java, to avoid having multiple source files (i.e., *Publisher.java, Bakery.java*, etc.).

---

***Listing 9-1.*** *A Java implementation of Figure 9-2 demonstrating inheritance (filename Business.java)*

```java
// Define abstract base class
abstract class Business {
// Define class attributes/variables
public double turnover = 20000;
public String address = "none";
// Define method for displaying address attribute/variable
void DisplayAddress() {
 System.out.println(address);
}
    // Create main method
    public static void main(String[] args)
    {
    // Uncommenting the next line will throw an error
    // Business business1 = new Business();
    // Create new Bakery object, happybakery, and display its address
    Bakery happybakery = new Bakery();
    System.out.println("A new bakery is opened at " + happybakery.address);
    // Create new FictionPublisher object, jolly_books, and display its
    turnover
    FictionPublisher jolly_books = new FictionPublisher();
    System.out.println("Fiction publisher Jolly Books had an unfortunate
    turnover of £" + jolly_books.turnover + " in 2020");
    // Create new NonFictionPublisher object, silly_books, set and display its
    turnover
    NonFictionPublisher silly_books = new NonFictionPublisher();
    System.out.println(("Non-fiction publisher Silly Books had a great turnover
    of £" + (silly_books.turnover + " in 2020")));
    // Create new LuxuryPerfumerie object, exquisite_odors, set and display its
    address
    LuxuryPerfumerie exquisite_odors = new LuxuryPerfumerie();
    exquisite_odors.address = "10 Wacky Avenue";
    System.out.print("A wonderful luxury perfumerie is located at ");
    exquisite_odors.DisplayAddress(); // Summon method inherited from
                                      Business class
```

```
    }
}
// Define the rest of the classes
class Bakery extends Business { String address = "2 Happy Street"; }
class WeddingBakery extends Bakery { }
class Perfumerie extends Business { }
class LuxuryPerfumerie extends Perfumerie { }
class Publisher extends Business { }
class FictionPublisher extends Publisher { double turnover = 4.55; }
class NonFictionPublisher extends Publisher { /* turnover is inherited from
Business class */ }
```

# Figure 9-2 in C#

Let's observe an implementation of Figure 9-2 on C# next. Like you may remember from previous chapters in this book, Java and C# are rather similar languages.

*Listing 9-2. A C# implementation of Figure 9-2 demonstrating inheritance*

```
using System;
abstract class Business {
    //  Define class attributes/variables
    public double turnover = 20000;
    public string address = "none";
    // Define method for displaying address attribute/variable
            void DisplayAddress() {
            Console.WriteLine(address);
            }
// Create main method
public static void Main() {
            // Uncommenting the next line will throw an error
            // Business business1 = new Business();
        //  Create new Bakery, happybakery, and display its address
        Bakery happybakery = new Bakery();
        Console.WriteLine("A new bakery is opened at " + happybakery.address);
        // Create new FictionPublisher, jolly_books, and display its turnover
        FictionPublisher jolly_books = new FictionPublisher();
        Console.WriteLine("Jolly Books had an unfortunate turnover of £"
        + jolly_books.turnover + " in 2020");
                // Create NonFictionPublisher, silly_books, set and display its
                turnover
                NonFictionPublisher silly_books = new NonFictionPublisher();
                Console.WriteLine("Silly Books had a great turnover of £"
        + silly_books.turnover + " in 2020");
```

```
    // Create new LuxuryPerfumerie, exquisite_odors, set and display its address
        LuxuryPerfumerie exquisite_odors = new LuxuryPerfumerie();
        exquisite_odors.address = "10 Wacky Avenue";
        Console.Write("A wonderful luxury perfumerie is located at " );
exquisite_odors.DisplayAddress(); // Summon method inherited from Business
class
        }
}
// Create the rest of the classes
class Bakery : Business { new public string address = "2 Happy Street"; }
class WeddingBakery : Bakery { }
class Perfumerie : Business { }
class LuxuryPerfumerie : Perfumerie { }
class Publisher : Business { }
class FictionPublisher : Publisher { new public double turnover=4.55; }
class NonFictionPublisher : Publisher { /* turnover is inherited from Business
class */ }
```

Listings 9-1 and 9-2 are nearly identical. For one, classes are implemented in a very similar fashion in both Java and C#. Naturally, there are a few differences (see Table 9-1).

**Table 9-1.** The main differences between Listings 9-1 and 9-2

| Element | Listing 9-1 (Java) | Listing 9-2 (C#) |
|---|---|---|
| Class inheritance | *class Publisher extends Business { }* | *class Publisher : Business { }* |
| Main method | *public static void main(String[ ] args)* | *public static void Main( )* |
| Console output | *System.out.println( … )* | *Console.WriteLine( … )* |
| Member declaration | *double turnover = 4.55;* | *new public double turnover = 4.55;* |

# Figure 9-2 in Python

And now for something somewhat different. Let's take a glance at what Figure 9-2 might look in Python (see Listing 9-3). To use abstract classes in Python, we need to import a code module called *ABC*. We then make our base class, Business, inherit from this module. The line *@abstractmethod* is a so-called Python decorator. Like you might've guessed, it's there to tell us a method is to be considered abstract.

**Listing 9-3.** *A Python implementation of Figure 9-2*

```
# import code module for working with abstract classes, ABC
from abc import ABC, abstractmethod
# define classes, starting with an abstract Business class
class Business(ABC):
    def _init_(self): # set class attribute default values
        self.address = "none"
        self.turnover = 20000

    @abstractmethod # define abstract method
    def Display_Address(self):
        pass

class Publisher(Business):
    def Display_Address(self):
        pass

class Bakery(Business):
    def Display_Address(self):
        pass
    def _init_(self):
        self.address = "2 Happy Street"

class Perfumerie(Business):
    def Display_Address(self):
        pass

class FictionPublisher(Publisher):
    def _init_(self):
        self.turnover = 4.55

class NonFictionPublisher(Publisher):
    pass

class WeddingBakery(Bakery):
    pass

class LuxuryPerfumerie(Perfumerie):
    def _init_(self):
        self.address = "10 Wacky Avenue"
    def Display_Address(self): # override abstract method
        print(self.address)

happybakery = Bakery() # Create new Bakery object
print("A new bakery is opened at", happybakery.address)
jolly_books = FictionPublisher() # Create new FictionPublisher object
print("Jolly Books had an unfortunate turnover of £", jolly_books.turnover,
"in 2020")
```

```
silly_books = NonFictionPublisher() # Create new NonFictionPublisher object
print("Silly Books had a great turnover of £", silly_books.turnover, "in 2020")
exquisite_odors = LuxuryPerfumerie() # Create new LuxuryPerfumerie object
print("A wonderful luxury perfumerie is located at ", end = '')
exquisite_odors.Display_Address() # summon Display_Address-method
```

# A UML Bicycle

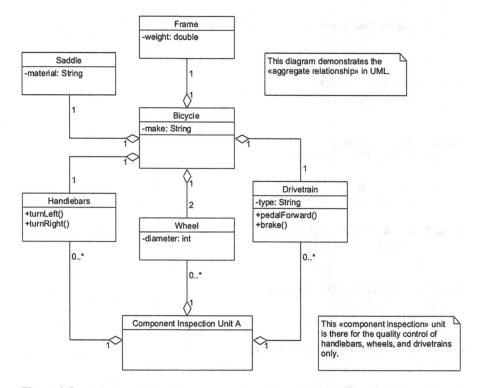

**Figure 9-3.** A diagram demonstrating aggregate relationships in UML

Next, let's explore how one could model a basic pedal-driven vehicle in UML. A new element is introduced in Figure 9-3. This is the *aggregate association*, portrayed by a hollow diamond symbol.

An aggregate association means a class can exist without other classes. To have a fully functional bicycle, we would need all of the components. However, the other components would still exist even if we were to remove them.

# A Bicycle in Python

Sticking to Python, let's create one possible programmatic interpretation of Figure 9-3 (see Listing 9-4).

***Listing 9-4.*** *A Python implementation of Figure 9-3 (i.e., a UML diagram for a* *bicycle). The Component Inspection Unit A is not implemented here for the sake of* *brevity*

```python
class Frame:
          # class constructor
          def __init__(self):
           print('Frame ready.')
          weight = 10.5 # define a class variable

class Saddle:
          # class constructor
          def __init__(self):
          print('Saddle installed.')
          material = "rubber" # define a class variable

class Drivetrain:
          # class constructor
          def __init__(self):
          print('Drivetrain installed.')
          type = "one-speed" # define a class variable

          # define class methods
          def pedalForward(self):
          print("Pedaling forward!")

          def brake(self):
          print("Braking!")

class Wheels:
          diameter = 0
          # class constructor
          def __init__(self, diameter):
          print('Wheels installed.')
          self.diameter = diameter

class Handlebars:
          # class constructor
          def __init__(self):
          print("Handlebars installed.")

          # define class methods
          def turnLeft(self):
          print("Turning left..")

          def turnRight(self):
          print("Turning right..")
```

```
class Bicycle:
            # define a class variable
            make = "Helkama"
            # set up class constructor & composition
            def __init__(self):
            self.my_Frame = Frame()
            self.my_Saddle = Saddle()
            self.my_Drivetrain = Drivetrain()
            self.my_Wheels = Wheels(571) # pass a new diameter value
            self.my_Handlebars = Handlebars()

def main(): # create main method
            # create Bicycle-object, "your_bike"
            your_bike = Bicycle()
            print("The wheels in your " + your_bike.make + "-bike are " +
            str(your_bike.my_Wheels.diameter) + " mm in diameter. The frame
            weighs " + str(your_bike.my_Frame.weight)+" lbs.")
            print("This bike has a " + your_bike.my_Drivetrain.type + "
            drivetrain and the saddle is made of the finest " + your_bike.
            my_Saddle.material+".\n")
            # summon class methods
            your_bike.my_Drivetrain.pedalForward()
            your_bike.my_Handlebars.turnLeft()
            your_bike.my_Drivetrain.pedalForward()
            your_bike.my_Handlebars.turnRight()
            your_bike.my_Drivetrain.brake()
if __name__ == "__main__":
            main() # execute main method
```

Question: How would you yourself interpret Figure 9-3 in Java and/or C#?

# A Personal Computer in UML

Let's now model something with both composite and aggregate associations. This is to have you contemplate scenarios in which you need to make a distinction between these two types of associations in UML.

Figure 9-4 represents a typical personal computer. It is meant to depict all the main components needed for a functional system. However, only some of these components are depicted using the composite association (i.e., the filled diamond symbol). This is because, in theory, one could have a personal computer up and running without them. It would not be the most useful system ever, but it would switch on and display error messages, at least.

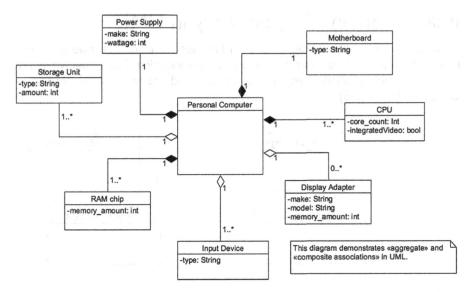

**Figure 9-4.** A diagram demonstrating composition relationships in UML

Essential computer components depicted with composite associations in Figure 9-4:

- Power supply, motherboard, CPU, and RAM chip(s)

Less essential components depicted with an aggregate association:

- Storage unit (e.g., a hard drive), input device (e.g., mouse and/or keyboard), and display adapter/video card (an integrated video chip may come with the CPU)

See Table 9-2 for a summary on the differences between aggregate and composite associations.

**Table 9-2.** The main differences between aggregate and composite associations in UML

| | Aggregate | Composite |
|---|---|---|
| Association strength | Weak | Strong |
| Relationship | "Has-a" | "Part-of" |
| Dependency | Subclasses can exist whether the superclass exists or not | Subclasses need a superclass to exist |
| Examples | Even when a class of *students* graduate, a *university* remains | *Rooms* are meaningless without a *house* |
| | Closing down a single *department* will not end the entire *corporation* | A functional *heart* is needed for a *human being* to live |

# Realization and Dependency in UML

Realization refers to a relationship with two sets of elements, one of which represents a *specification* and the other its *implementation*. The actual workings of an implementation depend on the context and are not strictly defined in UML (see Figure 9-5).

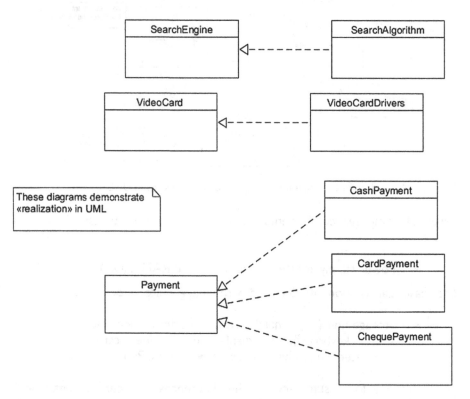

**Figure 9-5.** Three examples of simple realization relationships in UML

In the diagram in Figure 9-5, you'll see three simple examples of UML realization relationships. In the first one, a search algorithm provides the functionality for an online search engine. Similarly, video card driver software is needed for a video card to actually display any visuals. Finally, a payment event is made possible by three available types of payment method: cash, card, or check.

Next, we have the *dependency* (see Figure 9-6). This type of diagram denotes a connection between dependent and independent elements. Depicted using a dotted line and a simple arrowhead, dependencies are unidirectional in nature.

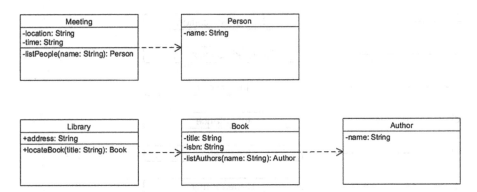

**Figure 9-6.** Two examples of UML dependency

# Reflexive Association

A *reflexive association* is there to represent instances belonging into the same class. When a class can be split into numerous responsibilities, we can use this type of association.

In Figure 9-7, we have a class called *Employee* with an association with itself as depicted by a now familiar simple line. The Employee class is used to represent both esteemed supervisors and lowly trainees; you'll notice UML multiplicity information is also inserted into this diagram.

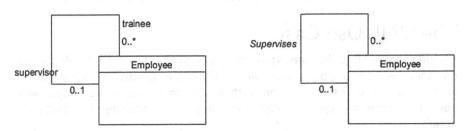

**Figure 9-7.** An example of a reflexive association in UML

Now, Figure 9-7 depicts the same setting in two different ways. The diagram on the left shows a *role-based* approach, as we do have the two different roles on display (i.e., supervisor and trainee). The right diagram uses a *named association*.

# UML Class Diagrams: The Basic Elements

At this point, it would be a good idea to review the elements of UML we've encountered so far (see Figure 9-8).

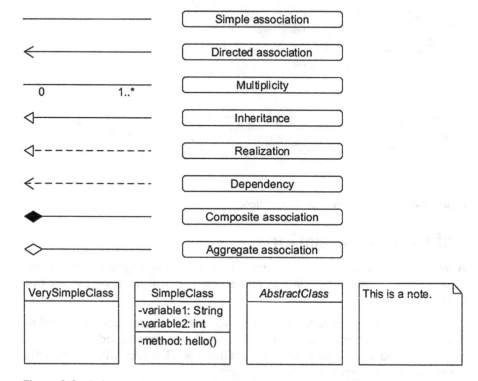

**Figure 9-8.** A diagram showing most of the basic elements used in UML class diagrams

# The UML Use Case

Although some UML diagram types are out of the scope of this book, there's one more you should be familiar with. This is the *use case*, which exists to demonstrate a user's interaction with a system in the most simple way possible. These are typically high-level diagrams containing few technical details.

We'll now introduce a few new UML elements. These are the *actor*, the *system*, and the *use case*. In addition, the use case diagram features familiar simple lines to depict relationships. Take a look at Figure 9-9 for a simple use case diagram.

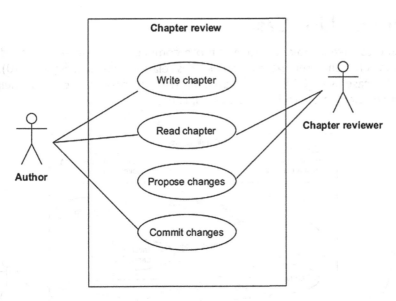

**Figure 9-9.** A UML use case depicting chapter review during a book-writing process

You'll see two actors in Figure 9-9, represented by some lovely stick figures. It's often a good idea to keep the actors categorical in nature as in naming an author *Author* instead of *John* or *Melody Woolysocks*. In UML, the actor initiating an interaction is known as a *primary actor*. A *secondary actor* is there to react to the actions of the primary actor.

The second element of *system* is represented by a simple rectangle in UML; in the case of Figure 9-9, it's called *Chapter review*. Inside the system, we have the inner *use cases*, denoted by oval shapes. These represent the different stages required to complete a specific use case. Finally, we have the familiar plain lines to represent the different associations of the actors and the use cases.

Now, the diagram in Figure 9-9 portrays the following sequence of events:

- **Author**, the primary actor, writes a chapter.

- The finished chapter is read by both the **Author** and a **Chapter reviewer**, the secondary actor. This is denoted by a shared association between the two actors.

- The Chapter reviewer proposes changes into the chapter.

- Finally, the Author commits changes into a chapter to end the scenario.

# More on Use Cases

It's time to take a look at a slightly more complicated use case to introduce two new elements: the *extends* and *includes* relationships (see Figure 9-10). As was the case with UML class diagrams, we can incorporate those helpful comment elements into UML use cases, too.

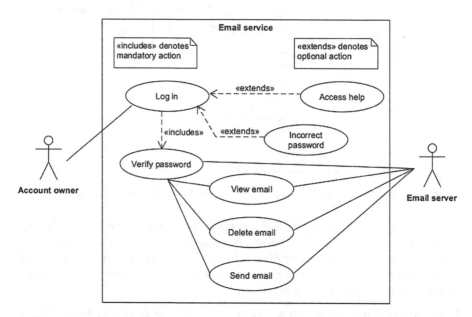

**Figure 9-10.** A UML use case depicting the basic functions of an email service

Figure 9-10 depicts a simple email use case scenario. We have the *account owner* (i.e., the human user) as the primary actor and an *email server* as the secondary actor. Figure 9-10 contains the following sequence of events:

- **Account owner** logs in with a password. If a wrong code is entered, an optional use case called *Incorrect password* is visited; this outcome is denoted with an arrow and the keyword <<extends>>.

- Account owner may also wish to read some help files. This, too, is an optional scenario and thus assigned with the keyword <<extends>>.

- A successful end result for the use case *Log in* automatically leads to another use case called *Verify password*, as depicted by the keyword <<*includes*>>. The secondary actor *Email server* is involved in the password authentication process, so a line of association is there in Figure 9-9 between said actor and the use case of *Verify password*.

- The use case Verify password leads to three more use cases: *View email*, *Delete email*, and *Send email*. Naturally, the secondary actor *Email server* is involved in all of these, too, although only in a passive role; Account owner initiates all of the three actions at their will.

---

Pay attention to the direction of your arrows when describing relationships in use cases.

---

# Tools for UML

Pen and paper aside, if you want to experiment with drawing UML and do so on your computer, there are plenty of great free options. We'll now review some of the finest examples of these tools.

## UMLet and UMLetino by UMLet Team

A free and wonderful open source tool, *UMLet* will have you drawing sassy class diagrams in no time with its intuitive drag-and-drop user interface. Association lines snap nicely onto class edges and stay there, making organizing your diagrams a breeze.

UMLet features ready-made selections of visual elements for class diagrams, use cases, timing diagrams, and many others. The program exports to many common image file formats, including PNG, GIF, and SVG. UMLet is an absolute must-have for those in need of a nice, clean UML design tool. All diagrams in this book were created with UMLet.

One interesting feature found in UMLet is its semi-automated diagram creation. By navigating to *File* ➤ *Generate Class Elements from Files or Directory*, you can set up the initial stage of your UML diagram. Unfortunately, UMLet has some issues with creating associations when using this feature.

UMLetino is a browser-based version of the same software. It features most of the features of its offline sibling. In addition, UMLetino has Dropbox integration for importing and exporting diagram files. However, the software only supports the output of PNG image files.

- Download **UMLet** for any Java-capable operating system from www.umlet.com

- Run **UMLetino** in any Java-capable browser at www. umletino.com/umletino.html

# Diagrams.net by Diagrams.net Team

Actively maintained by a dedicated team, *Diagrams.net* is a versatile open source tool available in both browser and desktop editions. No user registration is needed for the latter. Diagrams.net is intended for both basic UML work and for advanced users, having features like layers and "plugins" for added functionalities.

Formerly known as "draw.io", the software offers robust file format support when exporting your UML diagrams, including Adobe PDF. Not only that, by selecting *File* ➤ *Export as* ➤ *Advanced*, you get to set attributes such as DPI (dots per inch) and border width.

- Download the desktop app for **Diagrams.net** from https://github.com/jgraph/drawio-desktop/releases

- Run **Diagrams.net** on your browser at https://app.diagrams.net

# Umbrello by Paul Hensgen and Umbrello UML Modeler Authors

Being in development since 2001, *Umbrello* is a great tool for any type of UML work. The software has an intuitive user interface as well as the option to generate code from UML. Umbrello can export your diagrams into (usually) functional Java, C#, Python, and many other programming languages; simply navigate to *Code* ➤ *Code Generation Wizard,* set your options, and click *Next.* The software also offers excellent formatting features, including having all of your operating system fonts available for the diagrams you're working on.

Don't let the garish default color scheme fool you—Umbrello is a highly useful application for many types of diagrammatic work.

- Download the desktop app for **Umbrello** from https://umbrello.kde.org

# In Closing

Finishing this chapter, you have gained knowledge on the following:

- The basic elements of UML class and use case diagrams
- How to translate simple UML diagrams into Java, C#, and Python

# Afterword

And so we reach the end of this book. The programming jargon which you might've found daunting in the past has become less intimidating. By now, variables, classes, and objects have become at least somewhat familiar concepts to you. You know how to make simple text-based applications in Java, C#, and Python. Perhaps you can even casually explain Python's strict requirements for indentation at parties. But your journey as a programmer is far from over. Knowing the building blocks of coding in three languages, you can now start gaining more experience in the field. A world of problem-solving awaits you.

Programming can be frustrating. But there's something uniquely satisfying in getting a pesky, nonfunctional listing to finally work. Whether you end up coding in a professional context or not, programming may become a kind of constructive addiction at some point. It can also be a wonderful cure for insomnia and/or boredom.

It takes a lot of intent and time to manifest meaningful coding projects, whether they are video games or atomized programming tasks defined by one's employer. But no line is wasted as you grow as a programmer. Even error messages can teach you the most valuable things.

*Ada Lovelace*, the love child of *Lord* and *Lady Byron*, is considered one of world's first programmers. She worked with several prominent scientists of her day, including *Charles Babbage* and *Michael Faraday*, at some point producing what is considered the first ever computer program. We'll let Ada have the last words:

> *I can throw rays from every quarter of the universe into one vast focus.*
> *My course is so clear and obvious that it is delightful to think how straight*
> *it is.*

—Ada Lovelace (1815–1852)

# Index

**I**

# A

Abstraction, 15, 46

Access modifiers, 53–55

American Standard Code for Information Interchange (ASCII), 9

Architecture implementation, 30

Asynchronous programming model (APM), 125

Asyncio module, 98–99

# B

Bit-derived units, 31

# C, D

Central processor units (CPUs), 2, 64

Computing architecture, 29–30

Console applications vs. graphical user interface (GUI), 36

Constructor methods, 50–51

Cooperative multitasking, 98

C# (sharp) programming language
access modifiers, 54–56
asynchronous processing, 124–127
binary digits, 14
BinaryWriter/BinaryReader classes, 113
calendar class, 109–110
classes, 24, 55
coding structure, 21

comparison operators, 20–21
compiling process, 15
CultureInfo class, 110–112
curly brackets/variable scope/code blocks, 21
dates/calendars, 107–108
declarations, 21–22
FileInfo class, 114–118
file manipulation, 112–114
for-loops, 25–26
garbage collection, 119
integrated development environments, 35
interpreted languages, 15
join method, 124
key differences, 23–24
MonoDevelop, 37
multithreading, 119–120
namespaces, 24
native vs. managed heap, 119
objects, 48
protected access, 57
sleep vs. yield method, 122–123
static/public methods, 49–50
System.Globalization namespace, 109
TAP design pattern, 125
TextWriter/TextReader classes, 112
thread locking/accessing, 121–122
ThreadPool, 124
UML implementation, 151–152
universal chatting simulator, 137–141
variables, 16
while-loop, 26

# E

Eclipse project, 32–34

Encapsulation, 46–47

Event-based asynchronous
pattern (EAP), 125

# F

File operations, 63
attributes query/deletion, 77–78
calendar, 80–82
display dates, 78–79
empty text file, 74
internationalization/localization, 83–84
Java, 74–75
leap years/time, 79–80
text-file creation/access, 75–76

# G

Garbage collection (GC), 119

Global interpreter lock (GIL), 94–95

Graphical user interface (GUI) vs. console
application, 36

# H

High-level/low-level languages, 15

# I

Inheritance, 45

Integrated development environments
(IDEs), 29
64-bit computing, 32
bit-derived units, 31
bug clustering, 41
C#, 35
code simplification, 41
computing architecture, 30–31
console applications vs. GUI, 36
debugging, 39–40
eclipse project, 33
IEC-based data storage units, 31
Java development, 32
methods, 40
MonoDevelop, 37
multitasking, 32
operating system, 32

post-mortem, 41
PyCharm, 38–39
remote debugging, 41
software bug, 39
testing process, 40
tracing/print, 40
Visual Studio installation, 35
workloads, 35

International Electrotechnical
Commission (IEC), 31

Internationalization, 83–84

Iteration, 25

# J, K

Java, 13
attributes query/deletion, 77–78
binary digits, 14
block/lock-based synchronization, 69
calendar, 80–82
checked/unchecked, 73–74
classes/OOP, 24
coding, 21
comparison operators, 20–21
compiling process, 15
curly brackets/variable scope/code
blocks, 21
customized date symbol creation, 81
date retrieval/formatting, 79
declarations, 21–22
environment development, 32
file operations, 74–75
for-loop, 26
internationalization/localization, 83–84
interpreted languages, 15
leap years/time, 79–80
multithreading, 63–65
objects, 48
programming code, 22–23
protected access, 57
static/public methods, 49–50
text-file creation and access, 75–76
throw statement, 72–73
time pattern–formatting, 79
try-catch blocks, 71
UML implementation, 150–151
universal chatting simulator, 141–144
variable, 16
while-loops, 25–26

Java Development Kit (JDK), 48

Java Runtime Environment (JRE), 48

Java Virtual Machine (JVM), 48

Join method, 124

## L

Linux
    eclipse project, 34
    MonoDevelop, 37
    PyCharm, 38

Localization, 83

## M

Mechanical hard drives, 3

Metacharacters, 91–93

Metric units, 31

Multiprocessing *vs.* multithreading, 95

Multithreading
    checked and unchecked, 73–74
    checkFruit() method, 72
    concurrency, 63
    C# sharp, 119–120
    error messages, 72
    exception handling, 70
    fairness, 68
    hyper-threading, 64
    implementation, 65
    lock property, 68
    processor cores, 64
    runtime exceptions, 73
    simplified diagram, 67
    starvation, 68
    synchronization, 68–69
    thread life cycle, 65–67
    throw statement, 72–73
    try-catch block, 70–71

## N

Native *vs.* managed heap, 119

Neutralmoods/badmoods/chatmoods, 132–133

## O

Object-oriented programming (OOP), 24–43
    abstract classes, 45
    access modifiers, 46, 53–54

C# access modifiers, 54–56
    classes/inheritance/UML, 44
    constructor, 50–51
    encapsulation, 46–47
    geezer class, 47
    getName method, 47
    JDK/JRE/JVM, 48
    object, 48
    overloading method, 52–53
    procedural paradigms, 44–45
    protected access, 57
    Python, 57–61
    setName method, 47
    static/public methods, 49–50
    unified modeling language, 56

Overloading methods, 52–53

## P, Q

Parallel processing, 94

Procedural/object-oriented programming
    languages, 44–45

Programming
    algorithms, 7
    ASCII, 9
    boilerplate code, 10
    central processing unit, 2
    definition, 1
    file format, 9
    flowcharts, 7
    full stack, 10
    gadgets/hardware, 1
    hard drive, 3
    hardware components, 2
    input/output, 6
    motherboard, 5
    random access memory, 4
    requirements, 5
    routine, 9
    software projects, 10
    source code, 8
    syntax, 8
    video cards, 3

PyCharm, 38–39

Python
    access modes, 86
    asynchronous event loop, 99–100
    asyncio module, 98

Python (*cont.*)
    attribute binding, 60–61
    attributes, 87
    binary digits, 14
    classes/OOP, 24
    comparison operators, 20–21
    compiling process, 15
    concurrent programming, 100
    data types, 17
    date-time module, 89
    directory/folder operations, 88
    file operations, 86–87
    for-loops, 25
    globbing, 89
    group()/sub() methods, 93–94
    implicit/explicit, 19
    inheritance, 59–60
    interpreted languages, 15
    iterables/generators/coroutines, 98
    lambda functions, 101–102
    loop, 26
    manipulate values, 18
    metacharacters, 91–93
    multiprocessing *vs.* multithreading, 95–97
    object-oriented programming, 57–61
    parallel processing, 94
    pattern matching, 88
    programmatic interpretation, 154–156
    PyCharm, 38–39
    RegEx functions, 93
    regular expression, 90–91
    searching, 89
    sleep() method, 134
    threading module, 96
    typecasting functions, 19
    UCS (see Universal Chatting Simulator)
    UML implementation, 153–155
    unzipping, 103
    variables, 16–18
    visualization, 97
    zip function/software, 102–105
Python Package Index (PyPI), 130–132

**R**

Random access memory (RAM), 4

**S**

Sleep *vs.* yield method, 122–123

**T**

Task-based asynchronous pattern (TAP), 125
Threads
    C# sharp, 121–122
    multithreading (see Multithreading)
    methods, 69–70
    synchronization, 67
Tree-based approach, 148

**U**

Unified Modeling Language (UML), 56
    aggregate association, 154, 157
    behavioral diagrams, 146
    book-writing process, 161
    categories, 146
    C# implementation, 151–152
    class/object diagram, 147–148, 160
    composite associations, 157
    computer components, 157
    Diagrams.net, 164
    email service, 162
    events, 161
    inheritance, 148–149
    Java implementation, 150–151
    object-oriented paradigm, 145
    personal computer, 156–157
    programmatic interpretation, 154–156
    Python implementation, 153–155
    realization/dependency, 158–159
    reflexive association, 159
    structural diagrams, 146
    tools, 163
    tree-based approach, 148
    Umbrello, 164
    UMLet/UMLetino, 163–164
    use cases, 160–163
Universal Chatting Simulator (UCS)
    capitalization, 134–135
    code modules, 130
    C# sharp
        console-based quiz program, 139–141
        file operations/threading, 140
        threading process, 137–139
    features, 130
    indomitable main loop, 133
    Java
        Delicious Finnish Recipes, 141–142
        stopwatch program, 143–144

neutralmoods/badmoods/chatmoods, 132
  score keeping, 135–137
Universal Modeling Language (UML), 44

## V

Video cards, 3–4
Visual Studio
  developer account/benefits, 36
  installation process, 35
  MonoDevelop, 37
  Windows/macOS, 35
  workloads, 35

## W, X

Windows/macOS
  hard drives, 3
  operating system, 32
  PyCharm's installation
    process, 38
  Visual Studio, 35

## Y, Z

Yield method, 122–123

Printed in the United States
by Baker & Taylor Publisher Services

Printed in the United States
by Baker & Taylor Publisher Services